THE BHAGAVAN-MAHIMĀ — THE HINDŪ SCRIPTURES
VOLUME I

भगवन्महिमा — खण्ड ।

य एतं देवम् एकवृतं वेद ।
स सर्वस्मै वि पश्यति यच् च प्राणति यच् च न ।
तमिदं निगतं सहः स एष एक एकवृद् एक एव ।
सर्वे अस्मिन् देवा एकवृतो भवन्ति ।

To him who knows, there is only one God.
All deities are but different names of the One.
He is the One, the only One.
He is the One who oversees what breathes and what does not breathe.
He is the One with all the power and the authority.

Atharvavēda *13-4-15, 19, 20, 21*

THE VĒDAS

वेद

Introduction and Translation
by
Āṅgirasa Muni

1999
Sacred Books, Inc.

First Printing March 1999

Publisher:
Sacred Books, Inc.
P. O. Box. 11388
Fort Wayne, IN 46857-1388

ISBN 1-893152-00-6
Library of Congress Catalog Card Number 98-090786

Composed by Devendra Agarwal, A-704, Sector C, Mahanagar, Lucknow, India
Printed in the U.S.A.

Ṛgvēda	ऋग्वेद
Yajurvēda	यजुर्वेद
Sāmavēda	सामवेद
Atharvavēda	अथर्ववेद

Contents

Acknowledgement 11
The Hindū Scriptures 15

Bookwise

I. The Ṛgvēda 39
II. The Yajurvēda (Vājasanēyī Saṃhitā) 143
III. The Sāmavēda 177
IV. The Atharvavēda 181

Subjectwise

1. Agni - the Messenger, the Priest, the Angel 225
2. Blessing 226
3. Business 228
4. Charity 229
5. Contentment 231
6. Creation 232
7. Death 234
8. Devotion 235
9. Dharma 237
10. Divinity in Man 238
11. Faith in God 239
12. Fearlessness 240
13. Forgiveness 242
14. Friendliness 243
15. Gambling 244
16. Gāyatrī Mantra 245
17. God 246
18. Good Deeds 254
19. Good Life 255

20. Health & Long Life 258
21. Home 260
22. Love & Unity 262
23. Mṛtyuñjaya Mantra 265
24. Peace Invocation 266
25. Prayers asking God for Favors 267
26. Ruler of the Country 271
27. Śaṃ Nō Dēvī Mantra 272
28. Service of Humanity 273
29. Sin, Repentence and Purification 274
30. Social Wisdom - Working together in Harmony 277
31. Speech 278
32. Śrī Rāma 280
33. Strength & Victory 281
34. Suicide & Killing of Conscience 282
35. Thankfulness 283
36. Virtue 284
37. Wedding Ceremony 287
38. Welfare & Prosperity 292
39. Widow 295
40. Wisdom 296
41. Work Ethic 299
Appendix 1. The Vēdas - Their Components 300
Appendix 2. The 33 Vedic Deities (Dēvas) 303
Appendix 3. List of Mantras Included 307
Appendix 4. Significant Dates 316
Appendix 5. The Transliteration of Dēvanāgarī Script to Roman Script and pronunciation 318

Acknowledgement

Thirty thousand hours of my life were, clearly, not enough to complete the monumental task of producing the Hindū scriptures and ancillary books in English language. I needed the time of many scholars for critiquing my manuscripts, removing the deficiencies and errors, and supplementing where necessary. I have received tremendous help. Their knowledge and wisdom have immensely increased the authenticity of these volumes. These persons have collectively spent approximately 16,000 hours in going over my manuscripts very minutely. I am grateful.

Dr. Purushottam Lal Bhargava, the scholar of Saṃskṛta, Ancient India, and Hindū scriptures, has very kindly heard the contents of all the volumes, except Rāmāyaṇa. He is, easily, one of the most learned men living. Going to him for help can be likened to going to the holy river Gaṅgā, a dip into which removes the impurities. His contribution to the quality of these volumes cannot be described in words. Āṅgirasa Muni is ever grateful to him. Reading out these scriptures to him and noting down his suggestions for improvement has taken five months. Sometimes he was, perhaps, not given enough time and was hurried through. For this reason, the responsibility for any deficiencies which have escaped are entirely those of Āngirasa Muni.

Dr. Shivani Mishra has painstakingly read all the volumes except Rāmāyaṅa and has made countless valuable suggestions for improvement of the texts. Her sincere dedication and meticulous attention to detail have proved invaluable in improving the quality of these volumes. She has helped immensely in the translation of the volumes on the Vēdas and the Upaniṣads into Hindī language. Her help is gratefully acknowledged.

Dr. Ramā Bhargava has gone over the Rāmāyaṇa volume in extreme detail and has held numerous discussions on how best to serve the reader of this volume. She has undoubtedly given her learning and wisdom not only to detect the errors of interpretation but also to improve the faithfulness of the translation to the original. She has also greatly helped in making the text of the original as authentic as possible. Mrs. Uma Bhargava has reviewed the Hindī translation by Dr. Ramā Bhargava.

Dr. Archana Srivastava has worked for several years to translate from English to Hindī the volumes of Śrīmad Bhāgavata & Mahābhārata and has, during this process, helped in improving the life-story of our Lord, Śrī Kṛṣṇa, by suggesting additions and deletions basing these on the two books. Mrs. Pūnam Bhargava and Dr. Rashmi Trivedi have also contributed to improving this volume.

Dr. Archana Srivastava has helped in the preparation of the Hindi version of The Bhagavad-Gītā.

Dr. Nod Nath Mishra has worked on the volume on Dharmaśāstra helping in the translation of Saṃskṛta texts into Hindī and Hindī or English texts into poetry form in Saṃskṛta. the poetic rendering of Āṅgirasa-smṛti in Saṃskṛta is his contribution to the volume. He has helped in making selections out of Manusmṛti.

Dr. Trilokanatha Jha has gone over the manuscript of the Āṅgirasa Dictionary of Hindū Religion, Culture, and Language several times and has corrected numerous errors. He has also written several articles for the Dictionary. He has reviewed the manuscript of The Āṅgirasa Gṛhyasūtra.

Mrs. Sunita Sharma has painstakingly interviewed people from different States and cultures of India in order to collect and write material for Āṅgirasa Gṛhyasūtra and the book titled Hindū Festivals and Pūjā. She has patiently worked on preparing the list of suitable names for Hindū boys and girls.

My daughter Mrs. Mala Steffen, and my daughter-in-law Mrs. Marina Bhargava have corrected numerous errors of language.

Dr. Shivani Mishra, Dr. Rama Bhargava, Dr. Archana Srivastava, Dr. Rashmi Trivedi, Dr. Nod Nath Mishra, Dr. Trilokanatha Jha, and Mrs. Sunita Sharma have spent several years towards improving these works.

In the volume on the Upaniṣads, the discussion on Śaṅkara and Rāmānuja is based on George Thibaut's Introduction to his translation of the Vēdāntasūtra. The statement that Sāmavēda has exactly 100 original mantras is based on the painstaking compilation of Dr. Śripāda Dāmodara Sātavalekara.

The author is grateful to all of the above and to God for creating such dedicated people. I am grateful to God who gave me the years and the desire to find Him.

Āṅgirasa Muni

The Hindū Scriptures

I. General Introduction

Scriptures are works which impart spiritual wisdom. Even though mankind has made significant advances in the field of science and knowledge during the past five thousand years, there is little evidence that there has been a noticeable increase in spiritual wisdom. Though human beings have achieved impressive material progress, the realization of God — the Supreme Soul, and of our own indwelling spirit have remained unachieved for most. As a result there is much misery and unhappiness evident in our world.

With the advances in our knowledge of the universe, man's need for spiritual wisdom has not diminished. Ever since men have been thinking of God, they have realized that spiritual wisdom does not come from scientific discovery but from faith in the Almighty and from a reverential study of the scriptures.

The Need for Dharma

Dharma is a much more comprehensive word than religion. Religion defines the personal relationship of man to God. Dharma defines his whole being. Dharma not only defines a person's relationship with God, it also determines how he should conduct his life in relation to the world. While in most religions of the world both aspects of dharma are emphasized, in Buddhism only the latter is. Even though in Buddhism God is not prayed to as such, Buddha is recognized as "pure enlightenment" or "perfect enlightenment". Perfect enlightenment comes very close to the concept of God in other religions.

Trust in God obtains for a person a just and supremely loving friend who is also supremely powerful. Trust in God helps a person accept life's troubles without complaint; it gives a person greater power and energy in pursuing desirable objectives; it allows a person to perform his duties with happiness; it gives a person the power to fight evil with greater confidence; and it persuades a person to give up his sinful ways and work for his own salvation.

Hindū Dharma

There are several religions in which the human population of the world is divided. The main religions are Hindū, Bauddha, Jaina, Sikh, Christian, Judaism, Islām, Shinto, Bahāi, Zoroāstrian, and Tāo. Besides the above there are some other religions with small following. Bauddha, Jaina, and Sikh religions are off-shoots of the Hindū religion and as such share many of the beliefs of the Hindūs. The Hindū Dharma is the oldest in the world, older than Judaism. Like the latter it was not established by a single person. Hindū religion was built collectively by hundreds of brilliant minds whose inspired statements created the Hindū scriptures.

The Name Hindū

The word Hindū is derived from the word Sindhu. The people living on the banks of the Sindhu River developed Hindū dharma and called themselves Sindhu people. That is where it all began. The religion of these people was called the Sindhu religion. In course of time Sindhu became Hindū. It is very common in that part of the world to pronounce s as h. Regardless of the origin of the word Hindū, now a native of any country, or a person of any race can call himself Hindū if he believes in Hindū dharma.

Principal Beliefs

All Hindūs are bound by certain strong fundamental beliefs which can be classified into 12 statements.

1. Hindūs believe in one God. This belief has been asserted numerous times in Hindū scriptures — in the Ṛgvēda and Atharvavēda, in all the Upaniṣads, and in Hindū philosophies of Nyāya, Vaiśēṣika, Yōga, and Vēdānta. Yet, because of the relationship of love with God, Hindūs are permitted to invent numerous names for God. This does not mean, as some non-Hindūs jump to conclude, that Hindūs believe in many Gods.

2. God is formless. He is neither male nor female. For this reason, all three pronouns - He, She, and It have been used for God in Hindū religious writings. Yet, Hindūs often represent God as a pair of male and female. When they refer to God, the life-giver they have male Brahmā and have with him female Sarasavatī who has the power to grant wisdom. When they refer to the sustainer Viṣṇu as the male they have with Him female goddess Lakṣmī who wields the power to grant prosperity. When they refer to beneficent Śiva as the male who is responsible for dissolution, they have with him Durgā who grants physical strength to people.

3. Śrī Rāma and Śrī Kṛṣṇa were two perfect human lives. Since only God can be perfect, Hindūs believe that in these two lives God himself descended into visible human form (avatāra).

4. There are three ways to reach God — through knowledge, action, and devotion (jñāna, karma, and bhakti).

5. Saṃskṛta language written in Dēvanāgarī script is the religious language of the Hindūs.

6. The word Ōm means "yes". It is sacred just like the word "Amen" in Christianity. It is written in a special way and is pronounced before and after a mantra. It has come to represent the Almighty God.

7. God is the Supreme Soul who lives in every human heart. The human body is, therefore, the temple of God and should not be desecrated by sinful deeds.

8. God ordains human beings to live a life of truth, righteousness, charity, love, and service of mankind. Serving others is the highest religious act and giving pain to others the most irreligious act.

9. God gives us life, sustains us, and when the time comes, absorbs us back either into himself or sends us back to earth into a new life. As giver of life he is called Brahmā. As the all-pervading sustainer He is called Viṣṇu, and the beneficent God who performs the function of dissolution is called Śiva. When God is remembered as the remover of obstacles and a loving friend, Hindūs call Him Gaṇapati. When God is remembered as the Granter of wisdom, Hindūs call the Almighty, Goddess Sarasvatī. When God is remembered as the Granter of prosperity, Hindūs call the Almighty, Goddess Lakṣmī. When God is worshipped as the perfection of incarnation in a human body Hindūs worship Him as either Śrī Rāma or Śrī Kṛṣṇa.

10. God rewards good deeds and punishes evil deeds. Forgiveness is not granted by mere asking. A person needs to be truly regretful of his sin and to say to God that he will henceforth lead a life of virtue. God, thereupon, may, in his mercy, consider his good deeds as offset to his evil deeds and thus save him from suffering. Man, however, does not have a right to be forgiven.

11. If a person has not been punished for all his evil deeds in his present life, his soul, upon his death, will carry the account to his next birth when he will be paid for what he did in his past lives. His deeds are called karma. The cycle of births continues because of his karma. The goal of a person is to get out of this cycle by continuously doing selfless deeds and asking God to grant him liberation from the cycle (saṃsāra). When this happens, the individual merges his identity in the Supreme Soul.

12. Svastika is the sacred symbol of Hindūs. The word is derived from su-asti essentially meaning "may all be well with you" This symbol is formed on a wall, floor, or any other suitable place to wish well. Hitler took it as the symbol of Ārya (Āryan) race as he declared Germans to be Āryans.

The Need for One Dharma

For thousands of years men have been behaving like naughty teenagers separating themselves into many religious groups with either the secret or open aim of claiming superiority over other men. The followers of many of these groups believe that God likes only those who belong to their religious group and disapproves those who belong to religious groups other than theirs. Members of some of the extremist religious groups believe that God wants them to plunder and destroy the people who belong to other religious groups.

Someday in the future when human beings grow out of adolescence they will believe in just one dharma. They will then cease to use religion as an excuse to form political groups for the sake of establishing their own supremacy. They will grow up to realize that all human beings regardless of color and geography are God's children and deserve respect. At this point there will be only one religion, one dharma, and one set of scriptures needed for the entire humanity. If and when this happens, mankind will achieve unity in its trust of, and obedience to, God.

The Role of the Hindū Scriptures

Although the scriptures of many other religions are being studied with benefit not only by the followers of the religion to which they belong but also by others, Hindū scriptures which have to contribute so much to the entire world, have, for the most part, not been studied.

The question may be asked: Why then have Hindū scriptures not taken hold and helped mankind to maturity in spiritual wisdom? The answer to this question is threefold. (1) These scriptures are in Saṃskṛta language and until the work of Āṅgirasa Muni no reliable translation in living languages was produced. (2) The scriptures have been mixed with extraneous matter by unauthorized interpolators to such an extent that the extraneous matter forms ninety percent of the material. This is very discouraging to the reader who wants to read only the scriptures. Lastly, (3) not only are all scriptures written in Saṃskṛta, most of them are written in extremely condensed form adding further difficulty in understanding them. This work in six volumes removes all these obstacles to reaching the Hindū scriptures.

Description of The Scriptures

In all, there are 30 books of Hindū scriptures. They are organized in six volumes as follows.

1. The four Vēdas;
2. The fourteen Upaniṣads;
3. The Bhagavad-Gītā;

4. The Rāmāyaṇa;
5. Śrīmad Bhāgavata & the Mahābhārata;
6. The eight Dharmaśāstra books.

1. The Four Vēdas

The Vēdas are the most ancient and the most revered of the Hindū scriptures. There are four Vēdas: Ṛgvēda, Sāmavēda, Yajurvēda, and Atharvavēda. Ṛgvēda, the oldest and the most important of the four Vēdas, was composed during the 3000-1100 BCE. period. The other three Vēdas were composed during the 2000-1100 BCE. period.

Subject-matter of the Vēdas

The verses of the Vēdas contain prayers which seek contentment, courage, energy, fearlessness, forgiveness, mercy, good life, happiness, health, immortality, intellect, long life, mental growth, mercy, peace, progeny, prosperity, purification, reward for virtue, righteousness, riddance from sin, success in general, success in business, victory, virtue, wealth, welfare, wisdom, and zeal. Besides these there are prayers singing the glory of God. There are yet others expressing repentance, and thankfulness. The Vēdas include prayers for special occasions including house-warming, wedding ceremony, and for the host in whose house people are gathered.

Although most of the verses take the form of direct or indirect prayers, many of the verses carry moral instruction on how God wants men to live their lives, or on how God created this universe and gave to mankind this generous earth. These verses dwell on the beginnings of the universe, the value of charity, death and after, discretion in speech, divinity in man, gambling addiction, goal of life, God's generosity, God's mercy, God's will, importance of harmony in the family, helping one another, idle talk, laziness, love, loyalty in marriage, maligning of others, man to woman, noble thoughts and actions, one God, recognition of God, service of others, sweetness in speech and behavior, unity, widowed woman, and work ethic.

2. The Fourteen Upaniṣads

The Upaniṣads are soul-stirring writings. They are a class of works embodying the greatest flowering of thought of all times in respect to God — the Supreme Soul, and human beings who are endowed with individual souls. They deal with the nature and purpose of existence, the ultimate reality, and the attainment of beatitude. The Upaniṣads establish the relationship of man to God. They point out that God is bigger than the biggest and subtler than the subtlest.

There are, perhaps, over one hundred so-called Upaniṣads, but only 14 of these, almost all of which were composed during 1100-700 BCE., contain scriptural material. They are the Aitarēya, Bṛhadāraṇyaka, Chāndōgya, Īśāvāsya, Kaṭha, Kaivalya, Kauṣītaki, Kēna, Maitrī, Māṇḍūkya, Muṇḍaka, Praśna, Śvētāśvatara, and Taittirīya Upaniṣads.

3. The Bhagavad-Gītā

Bhagavad-Gītā (Holy Dialog). This is one of the holiest scriptures of Hindū dharma. It is essentially a dialog between God (Kṛṣṇa) and man (Arjuna) in which Kṛṣṇa, the human incarnation of God, explains to Arjuna his duty as a person and his relationship with God. The sermon was delivered by Śrī Kṛṣṇa to Arjuna in 1100 BCE.. It was written down with some additions and alterations around 600 BCE. The Bhagavad-Gītā shows how to conquer your weaknesses and in so doing fill your life with joy. It explains the purpose of man on this earth. This is the book that lets you discover God in your own heart. In obeying the commandments of the Lord as enunciated in the Bhagavad-Gītā a person can achieve success, happiness, and salvation.

Devotion to Kṛṣṇa, the Lord in human incarnation, and to his message has the power of changing a person's life completely. It creates love in your heart for fellow human beings. Gītā trains its disciples in humility towards God and towards fellow human beings. Gītā's message is one of courage and belief in yourself. Gītā preaches action. You begin to know and realize strongly that your job is to do your duty and accept the results with a smile and without complaint. Gītā's message is that you are given the freedom to pursue the path of virtue or sin and the path of action or laziness. Yet each path has its consequences and the path of virtue and hard work is the path to God-realization.

4. The Rāmāyaṇa

Rāmāyaṇa is the life-story of Lord Śrī Rāma. This life-story was orally carried by bards for 1000 years until Vālmīki, in 650 BCE., wrote it in a book-form, in the Saṃskṛta language. This was the first complete life-story of Śrī Rāma. Since then the life-story of Śrī Rāma has been written by over 300 writers in different languages of the world. Special mention needs to be made of the ones written in Tamila by Kampan called Irāmāvatāram (1000 CE.) and in Avadhī by Tulasīdāsa called Rāmacaritamānasa (1600 CE.) It has been written in many East-Asian and South-east Asian languages, and in Tibetan.

5. The Bhāgavata and the Mahābhārata

Bhāgavata Purāṇa and Mahābhārata are the two most important of the 14 books as sources for the life-story of Lord Śrī Kṛṣṇa. The life-story of Śrī Kṛṣṇa appears in 12 Purāṇas viz. Agni, Bhāgavata, Brahma, Brahmāṇḍa, Brahmavaivarta, Garuḍa, Kūrma, Liṅga, Matsya, Padma, Vāyu, and Viṣṇu Purāṇa. Another book which is not called Purāṇa but is identical in style to the Purāṇas, and written around 400 CE. is Harivaṃśa. It also contains the life-story of Śrī Kṛṣṇa. Mahābhārata which began as a small book called Jaya in 1100 BCE. with 8800 verses, continued to be expanded until around 250 CE. it was finalized at approximately 98,000 verses and its name changed to Mahābhārata. On the basis of these 14 books the volume on the life of Śrī Kṛṣṇa has been prepared.

The Purāṇas

There are 18 main Purāṇas, 12 of which contain the life-story of Śrī Kṛṣṇa and 6 which do not. All of these came from one small Purāṇa written by Vēda Vyāsa in 1100 BCE. These 18 Purāṇas, perhaps 99% of the material of which does not constitute scripture, came about during the period 300 CE.-1000 CE. Unfortunately, the Hindū society was greatly influenced by these Purāṇas and began to believe that they were the real scriptures.

6. The Dharmaśāstra

Dharmaśāstra is a volume containing spiritual, moral, and worldly wisdom in the form of precepts. This volume is based on 8 books. Seven of the eight books written by Āpastamba, Baudhāyana, Bhartṛhari, Vasiṣṭha, Yājñavalkya, and the unnamed author of Manusmṛti, as also the Dhammapada, were written during 400 BCE. and 700 CE. The eighth book by Āṅgirasa Muni was written in 1998. These books guide an individual person towards achieving spiritual and worldly success and towards achieving happiness. They guide a society on how to attain high levels of morality, justice, and fairness, so as to benefit all of its members.

II. The Vēdas

As stated in the General Introduction there are four Vēdas. These were composed over a period of 1900 years starting 3000 BCE. and ending with 1100 BCE. During this period several families of ṛṣis (inspired sages) composed the hymns. These hymns were memorized and handed down from one generation to the next. It was in 1100 BCE. that Kṛṣṇa Dvaipāyana, popularly known as Vēda Vyāsa or Vyāsa, organized all the material into four volumes, dividing each book into chapters and each chapter into hymns. A hymn consists of several mantras in verse or prose form. The number of mantras in a hymn can vary significantly.

These four Vēdas are respectively Ṛgvēda, Yajurvēda, Sāmavēda, and Atharvavēda. Vyāsa divided the chapters of Ṛgvēda based on authorship rather than subject matter. For example, all the hymns composed by the descendants of Viśavāmitra were put in chapter 3 of the Ṛgvēda. The members of one family who composed these hymns had many mantras indentical with the mantras contributed by the members of other families. As a result there occurs a large duplication of material in each Vēda. Also Sāmavēda, consisting of 1875 mantras, was created largely as a selection of verses from the Ṛgvēda appropriate for singing or chanting. Yet 100 new mantras were composed for Sāmavēda. Yajurvēda and Atharvavēda contain, largely, original verses.

Each Vēda has a main book called Saṃhitā and three other ancillary sets of books called Brāhmaṇas, Āraṇyakas, and Upaniṣads respectively. Each Vēda can include more than one Brāhmaṇa, more than one Āraṇyaka, and more than one Upaniṣad. Most of the Brāhmaṇas and Āraṇyakas, if not all, have lost their religious usefulness over time. Upaniṣads, however, are a very valuable set of scriptures. Strictly speaking the term Vēda is supposed to mean the whole set of books as defined above, but in common parlance it is acceptable to call the Saṃhitā part the Vēda, for example Ṛgvēda Saṃhitā is called Ṛgvēda.

Authorship of the Vēdas

The oldest and the most important Vēda is Ṛgvēda. Even though the hymns of this Vēda were composed at widely different periods of time, the names of the authors have been preserved in the works called Anukramaṇīs. Most of these names seem credible. However, in the case of the other three Vēdas the names of the authors do not seem reliable.

Translations and Commentaries on Vēdas

Out of the four Vēdas the Ṛgvēda has received the most attention of the translators and commentators. Yāska (7th century BCE.) in ancient times and Sāyaṇa in medieval times (14th century CE.) are two of the most notable translators and commentators. In fact, Sāyaṇa who wrote his commentary in Saṃskṛta, forms the backbone of all the translations of Ṛgvēda which followed him in time. It is only through agreeing or disagreeing with Sāyaṇa that the later commentators and translators have been able to render their own versions. Sāyaṇa wrote his commentary on all four Vēdas.

While many people have worked on the Ṛgvēda, not much valuable work has been produced on the other three Vēdas. One notable name is that of Sātavalēkara who has done commendable work on all four Vēdas in the 20th century CE.

The Method of Selection of the Material

For the volume on the Vēdas all 20,500 pieces of prose and poetry were studied in order to choose which ones to include. The criterion was for a piece to be useful in enlightening the reader.

Vedic Hindūs and Their Outlook on Life

The Vēdas clearly reflect a period when people were full of radiant spirit. Their outlook on life was positive and optimistic. They felt good about their circumstance and asked for long life. The interest of the Vedic sages lay in this world rather than in the next. The Vedic Hindūs enjoyed the earthly life and prayed for wealth, health, and happiness in their prayers. They were valiant fighters and asked God to be on their side. They strongly believed in virtue and asked God to rid them of sin. They had a great regard for womanhood and defined the role of woman as equal to man in the society and family. They urged her to remarry upon becoming a widow.

To the Vedic people living a life of ṛta was necessary in order to please God. It is quite possible that the English words right and righteous are derived from the Saṃskṛta word ṛta. The Vedic Hindūs did not consider human beings to be essentially sinners. They considered man to be containing the germ of divinity. This belief of Vedic period travelled to the Upaniṣads and all the way into Buddhism.

"God created the heaven, the earth, and the man, and then entered the body of the man." (Atharvavēda 13-3-1)

Concept of God in the Vēdas

To Vedic Hindūs, God was Truth and Reality; and God was Ṛtavan, the defender of righteousness and moral order. God was all glory and beauty.

Names of God

The several hundred sages who contributed to the writing of the Vēdas addressed God by their own favorite names and forms. Each chose his favorite names and manifestations of God's power to pray to God. There are thirty three Dēvas in the Vēdas to represent God. Most of these names have lost their significance for even the Hindūs let alone non-Hindūs who would not be able to relate to these names at all. Mentioning these names would have not only created confusion but would have made the meaning difficult and purpose obscure for the reader. For this reason it was considered advisable to replace them by such words as Lord, Almighty, Supreme Being, Dēvas, or simply, God. It is believed that by doing so the message of the sages would be delivered more succinctly, without sacrificing faithfulness to the original.

One God or Many Gods?

Even though the Vēdas use so many names to pray to God, the sages who composed the Vēdas knew that even though God could be called by many names, there is only one power they are referring to, all the time, as is evident from the following:

"The one God they call by so many names..." (Ṛgvēda 1-164-46)

"...all life moving or stationery depends on One Supreme Being." (Ṛgvēda 3-54-8)

"The sage beholds the Being who dwells in us all and pervades the entire universe. In that Being is the union of all there is. This Being is the warp and woof of all creatures." (Yajurvēda 32-8)

"God is almighty. He is the one and only. In him all Dēvas become unified." (Atharvavēda 13-4-12/13)

"There are no eight, nine, or ten Gods. There are no five, six, or seven Gods. There are not even two, three, or four Gods. To him who knows there is only one God. All deities are but different names of the One. He is the One, the only One. He is the One who oversees what breathes and what does not breathe. He is the One with all the power and the authority." (Atharvavēda 13-4-15/21)

The belief in one God among Hindūs has persisted throughout the ages. Approximately 2700 years later when Manusmṛti was composed the author echoed the statement contained in the Ṛgvēda (1-164-46):

"He is the One. People call that eternal almighty God by different names ..." (M. 12-123)

Even today every Hindū knows that there are several thousand names by any one of which he could address God; but they all refer to the one Almighty. There is a remarkable cohesion among Hindūs and no quarrel as to the superiority of one name over the other.

The Ṛgvēda

Ṛgvēda is not only the oldest of the Saṃhitās, it is also the largest and the most important. It is the collective work of over 300 contributors. It consists of 1028 hymns, which altogether contain 10552 mantras in verse form. The mantras composed by 57 ṛṣīs were found most desirable to be selected in this volume.

Even though for hundreds of years the Vēdas remained only the spoken word, unwritten, and handed down by word of mouth, there is a remarkable identity of text throughout India for Ṛgvēda, as well as for Sāmavēda and Atharvavēda. Even though composed during the 3000-1100 BCE. Ṛgvēda consists of some of the best prayers ever composed by mankind in praise of God. One typical example:

"God! Be unto us easy of access, as is a father to his son. Be ever present in our midst giving us happiness." (Ṛgvēda 1-1-9)

Vedic Hindūs prayed to God to make them prosperous. The prosperity is desired not only to enjoy good life but also to take care of the less fortunate. The following is an outstanding example.

"I am desirous of prosperity for the sake of making generous gifts." (Ṛgvēda 1-185-9)

The Vedic people were very concerned that they should always follow the path of virtue. The prayers constantly ask God to make them virtuous and keep them away from sin.

"We shall follow the virtuous path steadfastly..." (Ṛgvēda 5- 51-15)

"God, ...we ask you to steer us away from the evil path, and put us on a course which has your blessings." (Ṛgvēda 5-82-5)

"O God! Forgive if I have ever committed sin against a benefactor, a dear friend, or a companion, or my own brother, or my neighbor, or a stranger. (Ṛgvēda 5-85-7)

"We may have committed sins against friends and family members. We repentantly pray to you for forgiveness because these are sins against you, O Dēvas." (Ṛgvēda 1-185-8)

Vedic Hindūs did not want to be helpless worshippers but instead wanted health and vigor to lead a life full of achievement and victory. The following hymns are two of several.

"When danger faces us from outside God wants us to face it by uniting together and by so doing to obtain victory."
(Ṛgvēda 1-179-3)

"Men! God has given you the elixir of life. Yet he is a friend of only those who work hard." (Ṛgvēda 4-33-11).

Besides prayers, Ṛgvēda also contains some excellent moral advice. For example,

"God withholds his favors from the rich person who is Godless and who is not interested in giving charity."
(Ṛgvēda 1-150-2)

Again, "If all speech could be divided into four equal parts, the wise will replace three parts with silence." (Ṛgvēda 1-164-45)

There is unlimited beauty of thought and expression in the hymns of Ṛgvēda. It will not serve much purpose in describing these any further. The way to get it all is to read the Ṛgvēda as published in this volume.

Sāmavēda

Sāmavēda consists of a total of 1, 875 mantras. If repetitions are not considered, the number reduces to 1,549. Of these only 100 are original. Out of 1,449 that are not original two (321 and 464) are borrowed from Yajurvēda Saṃhitā and 1447 are repetitions of Ṛgvēda mantras. From the original 100, Atharvavēda has borrowed two.

Yajurvēda

Yajurvēda has two major versions called Kṛṣṇa Yajurvēda and Śukla Yajurvēda respectively. Since literally Kṛṣṇa means dark and Śukla means fair, these versions are also called Black Yajurvēda and White Yajurvēda respectively, although white and black colors have nothing to do with the contents. Kṛṣṇa essentially means mixed material and Śukla suggests purified material. The process of purification suggests that Kṛṣṇa version was the original and the editor who prepared the Śukla version omitted the portions he deemed not very useful. In addition to this major difference between the two versions there are hundreds of minor textual differences between the two. Each of these major versions has more than one minor versions which differ very little from each other. They are called rescensions. Kṛṣṇa Yajurvēda has four rescensions of which the rescension called Taittirīya Saṃhitā is by far the most popular. Śukla Yajurvēda is also called Vājasanēyī Saṃhitā. It has two rescensions of which Mādhyandina rescension is the most popular. In South India Kṛṣṇa Yajurvēda is more popular and in the North the Śukla Yajurvēda.

Śukla Yajurvēda - Mādhyandina rescension consists of 2,086 mantras some of which have been borrowed from Ṛgvēda. Yet unlike Sāmavēda it is substantially an original composition. Again the spirit of positive attitude pervades the Yajurvēda much the same as it does the Ṛgvēda.

"Our earth! this our earth is immense; it provides us abundance; it is all sustaining - all nourishing. It has room for the entire mankind whom it so graciously supports. We can see clearly that our earth is not hostile to us." (Yajurvēda 13-18)

The Vedic Hindūs loved life and were desirous of enjoying their lives. This love is reflected in the prayers asking God for a life-span of 100 years and for God to give them perfect health till the end.

"... May we be granted a hundred years to live;
a hundred years to hear and see well;
a hundred years to speak clearly;
a hundred years of self-dependence; and
Yes, all of the above, and even in excess of hundred years.
(Yajurvēda 36-24)

The prayers of Yajurvēda not only seek favors from God, they also thank God for the gifts he has apportioned to mankind.

"God! The granter of welfare, the source of happiness, the beneficent, the cause of joy, the auspicious, and the source of bliss, salutations to you. (Yajurvēda 30-4)

Atharvavēda

The Atharvavēda consists of 5,987 mantras. It is a radical departure from the other three Vēdas. It is a later contribution relative to the other three. It has many themes other than prayers. It has many verses which are used for the performance of the wedding ceremonies because they relate to the union of man and woman. Then there are prayers for the new house and the new family. The verses of this Saṃhitā advocate unity and togetherness in the community and loving relationship in the family.

"Let the son be devoted to his father; Let him be of one mind with his mother; Let the wife be sweet and gentle to her husband."
(Atharvavēda 3-30-2)

The Vedic Hindūs of the period of Atharvavēda Saṃhitā were more modern from the standpoint of western standards than during the three thousand years that followed. Consider verse 9-5-27 which says:

"A woman may lose her husband to death. Such a woman may find a new husband and dedicate her love to the newlyfound mate.

The place of the Vēdas in the Hindū religion is so high that a person who does not believe in God and Vēdas is considered an atheist or a Non-Hindū. Secondly, when Hindūs want to call a statement perfect they call it "Vēdavākya" meaning it is like coming out of a Vēda. Both of these facts show how highly the Vēdas are revered by Hindūs. A reading of this volume will convince the reader that the Vēdas certainly deserve this exalted position among the Hindū scriptures.

The Responsibility of a Translator

When an author writes, he wants to convey his ideas, thoughts, moods, emotions, and feelings. Quite often the literature that lasts centuries is the one whose authors have successfully conveyed all these when saying important things. A translator's job is to bring the original author to the readers of a different language. It is imperative that the translator does not translate words but the ideas, thoughts, moods, emotions, and feelings of the original author. He must capture the soul of the original work. A translation which has not captured the soul of the original can be likened to a dead person. Let us take an example to illustrate the point. Assume that we were to translate the famous first verse of the Īśāvāsya Upaniṣad which states -

ईशा वास्यम् इदं सर्वं यत् किञ्च जगत्यां जगत्
तेन त्यक्तेन भुञ्जीथा मा गृधः कस्यस्विद् धनम् ।।

īśā vāsyam idam sarvam yat kiñca jagatyāṃ jagat
tena tyaktena bhuñjīthā mā gṛdhaḥ kasyasvid dhanam

The literal translation could read:

All this - whatever moves on the earth should be covered by the Lord. Protect (?) through detachment. Do not covet, for whose is wealth?

Reading of this literal translation will miss most of what this beautiful verse is saying. The real translation which captures both the meaning and the spirit of the original would state as follows:

In this changing world everything and everybeing is enveloped by God. Live in this world without attachment. Be happy in what has been apportioned to you and do not covet what rightly belongs to others.

There are certain Saṃskṛta words which cannot be translated because English equivalents are not available. Hence these Saṃskṛta words have been used in the hope that they will become part of the English dictionary in due course. For example, the words dharma, tapas, sattva, rajas, and tamas have no English equivalents. Wherever it was felt that a mere translation would not make the meaning lucid, a short commentary was added to help the reader.

The six volumes of Hindū scriptures translated from Saṃskṛta originals into English language convey the message of these scriptures. These volumes have omitted what is repetitive and what is non-scriptural.

Āṅgirasa Muni, the translator and commentator, has invested the equivalent of 40 years of work in preparing the comprehensive Hindū scriptures in English and other languages. In 5,000 years of Hindū civilization, since Manu Vaivasvata, the first recorded king of Hindū heritage, this is the first time that this monumental task has been done.

Whatever has been said here, including the chronology and dates, is based on scientific historical evidence, and not because some European or Indian scholar said so. It is hoped that these volumes will bring about a revolutionary awakening among Hindūs who will realize that their ancestors left them a diamond mine of which they were not fully aware. The time for enlightenment has arrived. Hindūs should not only now claim the wisdom stored in their own scriptures, but should share it with the rest of the humanity.

Āṅgirasa Muni

I

ऋग्वेद

The Ṛgvēda

Maṇḍala 1

Agni - the Messenger

अग्निम् ईळे पुरोहितं यज्ञस्य देवम् ऋत्विजम् ।
होतारं रत्न धातमम् ।　　　　|| ऋ. 1-1-1 || *

agnim īḷē purōhitaṃ yajñasya dēvam ṛtvijam
hōtāraṃ ratna dhātamam

I glorify Agni, the divine priest and the messenger of my oblations to God who is the bestower of prosperity.

अग्निः पूर्वेभिर् ऋषिभिर् ईड्यो नूतनैरुत ।
स देवां एह वक्षति ।　　　　|| ऋ. 1-1-2 ||

agniḥ pūrvēbhir ṛṣibhir īḍyō nūtanairuta
sa dēvāṃ ēha vakṣati

May Agni, the divine priest who is glorified by both the past and the present sages, increase and strengthen our bond with the Dēvas.

---

* The Ṛgvēda Saṃhitā is divided into maṇḍalas (chapters). Each maṇḍala is divided into several sūktas (hymns) and each hymn consists of several ṛcās or mantras. In the numbering of each mantra the first number refers to the maṇḍala, the second to the sūkta, and the third to the mantra itself.

Commentary

In this and many succeeding mantras the prayer addresses more than one Dēva. Since the sages considered Dēvas the various powers of God, they, in actuality, appealed to God through these powers.

Agni - the Priest

अग्निना रयिम् अश्नवत् पोषम् एव दिवे दिवे ।
यशसं वीरवत्तमम् । ।। ऋ. 1-1-3 ।।

agninā rayim aśnavat pōṣam ēva divē divē
yaśasaṃ vīravattamam

Praying to God through Agni, the angel priest, may we the worshippers obtain valiant offspring, and daily increasing prosperity and glory.

Prayer of Devotion

उप त्वाग्ने दिवे दिवे दोषावस्तर् धिया वयम् ।
नमो भरन्त एमसि । || ऋ. 1-1-7 ||

upa tvāgnē divē divē dōṣāvastar dhiyā vayam
namō bharanta ēmasi

O Lord, the remover of darkness!

We pray to you morning and evening with sincere thoughts of reverence. Through our prayers we come close to you.

Prayer Seeking Protection

स नः पितेव सूनवेऽग्ने सूपायनो भव ।
सचस्वा नः स्वस्तये । || ऋ. 1-1-9 ||

sa naḥ pitēva sūnavē'gnē sūpāyanō bhava
sacasvā naḥ svastayē

God! Be unto us easy of access, as is a father to his son. Be ever present in our midst, giving us happiness.

Prayer of Devotion

अथा ते अन्तमानां विद्याम सुमतीनाम् ।
मा नो अति ख्य, आ गहि । ।। ऋ. 1-4-3 ।।

athā tē antamānāṃ vidyāma sumatīnām
mā nō ati khya, ā gahi

O Lord! We recognize you amidst the enlightened persons. They are closest to you. We implore you not to pass us by. We ask you to come to us and give us enlightenment.

Prayer Seeking Good Life

स घा नो योग आ भुवत्, स राये, स पुरंध्याम् ।
गमद् वाजेभिर् आ स नः । ।। ऋ. 1-5-3 ।।

sa ghā nō yōga ā bhuvat, sa rāyē, sa puraṃdhyām
gamad vājēbhir ā sa naḥ

Lord! Help us attain our objectives. Help us acquire a sharp mind. Grant us food. Make us prosperous.

Prayer in Praise of God

केतुं कृण्वन्न् अकेतवे पेशो मर्या अपेशसे ।
समुषद्भिर् अजायथाः । || ऋ. 1-6-3 ||

kētuṃ kṛṇvann akētavē pēśō maryā apēśasē
samuṣadbhir ajāyathāḥ

Mortals! You owe your daily birth to the Lord, who with the rays of the morning Sun gives sense to senseless and form to formless.

Prayer Seeking Mercy

इन्द्रो दीर्घाय चक्षस आ सूर्यं रोहयद् दिवि ।
वि गोभिर् अद्रिम् ऐरयत् । || ऋ. 1-7-3 ||

indrō dīrghāya cakṣasa ā sūryaṃ rōhayad divi
vi gōbhir adrim airayat

To render all things visible, God elevated the Sun in the sky, and charged the clouds to produce abundant rain.

Prayer Singing Glory

परित्वा गिर्वणो गिर इमा भवन्तु विश्वतः ।
वृद्धायुम् अनु वृद्धयो, जुष्टा भवन्तु जुष्टयः ।।
।। ऋ. 1-10-12 ।।

paritvā girvaṇō gira imā bhavantu viśvataḥ
vṛddhāyum anu vṛddhayō, juṣṭā bhavantu juṣṭayaḥ

God! You deserve all the glory.

May we gain your full attention through loving prayers. May those who sing your praises receive your love.

Prayer Expressing Thankfulness

विभक्तारꣳ हवामहे वसोश् चित्रस्य राधसः ।
सवितारं नृचक्षसम् । ।। ऋ. 1-22-7 ।।

vibhaktāraṃ havāmahē vasōś citrasya rādhasaḥ
savitāraṃ nṛcakṣasam

Lord — the excellent and the beneficent!

We invoke you and thank you for the gifts which you have so graciously apportioned to us. You certainly watch over us.

Prayer Singing Glory

इदं विष्णुर् वि चक्रमे त्रेधा नि दधे पदम् ।
समूह्ळम् अस्य पांसुरे ।   ।। ऋ. 1-22-17 ।।

idaṃ viṣṇur vi cakramē trēdhā ni dadhē padam
samūhḷam asya pāṃsurē

In His stride the Lord (Viṣṇu) took three steps and the whole universe was collected in the dust of His feet. Hail to the Lord!

Commentary

The story of Bali and Vāmana incarnation of Viṣṇu was created later in the Purāṇas to explain the meaning of the three steps of Viṣṇu. Perhaps the Vedic seers considered the three steps of Viṣṇu as those of the Sun whose first step is to rise, second to span the globe, and the third to set.

Prayer Singing Glory

तद् विष्णोः परमं पदं सदा पश्यन्ति सूरयः ।
दिवीव चक्षुराततम् ।   ।। ऋ. 1-22-20 ।।

tad viṣṇōḥ paramaṃ padaṃ sadā paśyanti sūrayaḥ
divīva cakṣurātatam

O Lord Viṣṇu! The wise know that you are the omnipresent Supreme. You extend over and beyond the range of sky as the eye that can see everything.

Prayer Seeking Forgiveness

इदम् आपः प्र वहत यत् किं च दुरितं मयि ।
यद् वाहम् अभिदुद्रोह यद् वा शेप उतानृतम् ॥
॥ ऋ. 1-23-22 ॥

idam āpaḥ pra vahata yat kiṃ ca duritaṃ mayi
yad vāham abhidudrōha yad vā śēpa utānṛtam

My conduct may have been, at times, uncooperative and unjustifiably rebellious. I may not have spoken the complete truth, at times; and I may have used harsh language. I know that all this behavior is sinful. God! Let this water wash away from me this sinful behavior.

Prayer Seeking Wisdom

स नो विश्वाहा सुक्रतुर् आदित्यः सुपथा करत् ।
प्र ण आयूंषि तारिषत् । ॥ ऋ. 1-25-12 ॥

sa nō viśvāhā sukratur ādityaḥ supathā karat
pra ṇa āyūṃṣi tāriṣat

May the wise Lord keep us all our days on the righteous path and grant us long life.

Prayer Seeking Happiness

इमं मे वरुण श्रुधी हवम् अद्या च मृळय ।
त्वाम् अवस्युर् आ चके । || ऋ. 1-25-19 ||

imaṃ mē varuṇa śrudhī havam adyā ca mṛḷaya
tvām avasyur ā cakē

O Lord! Hear my prayer and invocation. Make this day a happy one. Protect me today.

Prayer in Praise of God

आ हि ष्मा सूनवे पितापिर् यजत्यापये ।
सखा सख्ये वरेण्यः । || ऋ. 1-26-3 ||

ā hi ṣmā sūnavē pitāpir yajatyāpayē
sakhā sakhyē varēṇyaḥ

O God! You give us the love of a loving father, the help of one who cares, and the friendship of a true friend.

Prayer Singing Glory

नकिरस्य सहन्त्य पर्येता कयस्य चित् ।
वाजो अस्ति श्रवाय्यः । ।। ऋ. 1-27-8 ।।

nakirasya sahantya paryētā kayasya cit
vājō asti śravāyyaḥ

O Almighty Lord!

Your power and reach are praiseworthy. No one dare harm your devotees.

Prayer Expressing Thankfulness

त्वमग्ने प्रमतिस् त्वं पिताऽसि नस्
त्वं वयस्कृत् तव जामयो वयम् ।
सं त्वा रायः शतिनः सं सहस्रिणः
सुवीरं यन्ति व्रतपामदाभ्य ॥
॥ ऋ. 1-31-10 ॥

tvamagnē pramatis tvaṃ pitā'si nas
tvaṃ vayaskṛt tava jāmayō vayam
saṃ tvā rāyaḥ śatinaḥ saṃ sahasriṇaḥ
suvīraṃ yanti vratapāmadābhya

O Loving God!

This whole world with its wealth belongs to you. You are the One who has given us life. You give us the love and protection of a father. You are our friend. You make us strong and brave. You defend the doers of virtuous deeds. You make it possible for men to acquire hundreds and thousands of material possessions.

Good men flock to you.

Prayer Seeking Protection and Strength

ऊर्ध्वो नः पाह्यंहसो नि केतुना विश्वं समत्रिणं दह ।
कृधी न ऊर्ध्वाञ्चरथाय जीवसे विदा देवेषु नो दुवः ।।
।। ऋ. 1-36-14 ।।

ūrdhvō naḥ pāhyaṃhasō ni kētunā viśvaṃ samatriṇaṃ daha
kṛdhī na ūrdhvāñcarathāya jīvasē vidā dēvēṣu nō duvaḥ

God! Make us walk erect. Protect us, by your splendor, from evil. Vanquish the evil. Allow us to make our journey through life saying our prayers to you.

Prayer Seeking Wisdom

उद् वयं तमसस् परि ज्योतिष् पश्यन्त उत्तरम् ।
देवं देवत्रा सूर्यम् अगन्म ज्योतिर् उत्तमम् ।।
।। ऋ. 1-50-10 ।।

ud vayaṃ tamasas pari jyōtiṣ paśyanta uttaram
dēvaṃ dēvatrā sūryam aganma jyōtir uttamam

O God Almighty! I am steeped into the darkness of ignorance. I need to be moved into the light of your wisdom.

Agni - the Messenger

नि काव्या वेधसः शश्वतस्कर् हस्ते दधानोनर्या पुरूणि ।
अग्निर् भुवद् रयिपती रयीणां सत्रा चक्राणो अमृतानि विश्वा ।।
।। ऋ. 1-72-1 ।।

ni kāvyā vēdhasaḥ śaśvataskar hastē dadhānōnaryā purūṇi
agnir bhuvad rayipatī rayīṇāṃ satrā cakrāṇō amṛtāni viśvā

The divine Agni, holds in His hands many good gifts for men. He conveys our prayers to the enternal Creator. The divine Agni bestows prosperity upon men.

Prayer Seeking Good Life

त्वमङ्ग प्रशंसिषो देवः शविष्ठ मर्त्यम् ।
न त्वदन्यो मघवन्नस्ति मर्डितेन्द्र ब्रवीमि ते वचः ।।
।। ऋ. 1-84-19 ।।

tvamaṅga praśaṃsiṣō dēvaḥ śaviṣṭha martyam
na tvadanyō maghavannasti marḍitēndra bravīmi tē vacaḥ

God! You are the mightiest. You can make us mortals happy. There is no one who can comfort men except you. We pray to you with these words of praise.

Prayer Seeking Protection

आ नो भद्राः क्रतवो यन्तु विश्वतोऽदब्धासो अपरीतास उद्भिदः ।
देवा नो यथा सदम्इद् वृधे असन्न प्रायुवो रक्षितारो दिवे दिवे ।।
।। ऋ. 1-89-1 ।।

ā nō bhadrāḥ kratavō yantu viśvatō'dabdhāsō aparītāsa udbhidaḥ
dēvā nō yathā sadamid vṛdhē asanna prāyuvō rakṣitārō divē divē

May auspicious powers exercise judgment in our favor. May the powers allowing us unobstructed pure life burst through in our favor. May the Dēvas always augment our family-welfare indeed. May the Almighty protect us day after day.

Prayer Seeking Prosperity and Long Life

देवानां भद्रा सुमतिर् ऋजूयतां
देवानां रातिर् अभि नो नि वर्तताम् ।
देवानां सख्यमुप सेदिमा वयं
देवा न आयुः प्र तिरन्तु जीवसे ।।
।। ऋ. 1-89-2 ।।

dēvānāṃ bhadrā sumatir ṛjūyatāṃ
dēvānāṃ rātir abhi nō ni vartatām
dēvānāṃ sakhyamupa sēdimā vayaṃ
dēvā na āyuḥ pra tirantu jīvasē

O Dēvas! Shower your benevolence upon us. May you be generous to us ever, approving of the righteous among us. May we obtain your friendship; and may you grant us long life.

Prayer Seeking Protection

तम् ईशानं जगतस् तस्थुषस् पतिं
धियं जिन्वम् अवसे हूमहे वयम् ।
पूषा नो यथा वेदसाम् असद् वृधे
रक्षिता पायुर् अदब्धः स्वस्तये ॥
॥ ऋ. 1-89-5 ॥

tam īśānaṃ jagatas tasthuṣas patiṃ
dhiyaṃ jinvam avasē hūmahē vayam
pūṣā nō yathā vēdasām asad vṛdhē
rakṣitā pāyur adabdhaḥ svastayē

He is the lord of what moves and what does not move. We invoke Him to protect us from what is evil (asat), to save us from decline and to support us in the growth of our mental abilities.

Prayer Seeking Welfare

स्वस्ति न इन्द्रो वृद्धश्रवाः स्वस्ति नः पूषा विश्ववेदाः ।
स्वस्ति नस् तार्क्ष्यो अरिष्टनेमिः स्वस्ति नो बृहस्पतिर् दधातु ।।
।। ऋ. 1-89-6 ।।

svasti na indrō vṛddhaśravāḥ svasti naḥ pūṣā viśvavēdāḥ
svasti nas tārkṣyō ariṣṭanēmiḥ svasti nō bṛhaspatir dadhātu

May Dēva Indra, the glorious, augment our welfare;
May Dēva Pūṣan, the all-knowing, augment our welfare;
May Dēva Sūrya, the protector from misfortunes, augment our welfare;
May Dēva Bṛhsapati, the granter of wisdom, augment our welfare.

Prayer Seeking Good Life

भद्रं कर्णेभिः शृणुयाम देवा भद्रं पश्येमाक्षभिर् यजत्राः ।
स्थिरैर् अङ्गैस् तुष्टुवांसस् तनूभिर व्यशेम देवहितं यदायुः ।।
।। ऋ. 1-89-8 ।।

bhadraṃ karṇēbhiḥ śṛṇuyāma dēvā
bhadraṃ paśyēmākṣabhir yajatrāḥ
sthirair aṅgais tuṣṭuvāṃsas tanūbhira
vyaśēma dēvahitaṃ yadāyuḥ

God!
May we listen with our ears to what is good;
May we see with our eyes what is good;
May we with firm limbs enjoy the term of life granted to us, singing your praises.

Prayer Seeking Health

शतम् इन्नु शरदो अन्ति देवा यत्रा नश्चक्रा जरसं तनूनाम ।
पुत्रासो यत्र पितरो भवन्ति मा नो मध्या रीरिषत् आयुर् गन्तोः ।।
।। ऋ. 1-89-9 ।।

śatam innu śaradō anti dēvā
yatrā naścakrā jarasaṃ tanūnāma
putrāsō yatra pitarō bhavanti
mā nō madhyā rīriṣat āyur gantōḥ

God! You have ordained hundred years as the life of man; please do not cut our life shorter.

Pray do not make us so infirm in our last years that we may need the paternal care of our children.

Commentary

The second part of the above mantra can be interpreted in the alternative, opposite meaning also: "Grant us old age in which we may depend on the paternal care of our children." Obviously, if this meaning is accepted, the prayer seeks for children who will serve the parents with loving care in their old age. In view of the spiritedness of the Vedic people, who vigorously aspired for personal freedom, this alternative meaning does not seem appropriate. Also Yajurvēda Saṃhitā mantra 36-24 reinforces our view that this prayer seeks non-dependence on children in old age.

Prayer Seeking Success and Joy

ऋजुनीती नो वरुणो मित्रो नयतु विद्वान् ।
अर्यमा देवैः सजोषाः । ।। ऋ. 1-90-1 ।।

ṛjunītī nō varuṇō mitrō nayatu vidvān
aryamā dēvaiḥ sajōṣāḥ

May Varuṇa, inspiring righteousness in us;
May Mitra, our friend and protector;
May Aryaman, calling us to remain active;
help us achieve our desires through straight (sinless) path,
and make our daily work joyful.

Prayer Seeking Reward for Virtue

मधु वाता ऋतायते, मधु क्षरन्ति सिन्धवः ।
माध्वीर्नः सन्त्वोषधीः । || ऋ. 1-90-6 ||

मधु नक्तम् उतोषसो, मधुमत् पार्थिवं रजः ।
मधु द्यौर् अस्तु नः पिता । || ऋ. 1-90-7 ||

मधुमान् नो वनस्पतिः, मधुमाँ अस्तु सूर्यः ।
माध्वीर् गावो भवन्तु नः । || ऋ. 1-90-8 ||

madhu vātā ṛtāyatē, madhu kṣaranti sindhavaḥ
mādhvīrnaḥ santvōṣadhīḥ

madhu naktam utōṣasō, madhumat pārthivaṃ rajaḥ
madhu dyaur astu naḥ pitā

madhumān nō vanaspatiḥ, madhumām̐ astu sūryaḥ
mādhvīr gāvō bhavantu naḥ

For us, your worshippers, who live righteously O Lord, let the breeze be fragrant; let waters in the rivers be sweet; let the herbs be potent; let our days and nights be happy; let the mother earth be sweet as honey; let the father heaven be like nectar; let our cows produce for us milk, sweet like honey; and let the sun be pleasant to us.

Prayer Seeking Welfare

शं नो मित्रः शं वरुणः शं नो भवत्वर्यमा ।
शं न इन्द्रो बृहस्पतिः शं नो विष्णुर् उरुक्रमः ।।
।। ऋ. 1-90-9 ।।

śaṃ nō mitraḥ śaṃ varuṇaḥ śaṃ nō bhavatvaryamā
śaṃ na indrō bṛhaspatiḥ śaṃ nō viṣṇur urukramaḥ

May Mitra, our friend and protector, be propitious to us.

May Varuṇa, the inspirer of righteousness, be propitious to us.

May Aryaman, calling for activity, be propitious to us.

May Indra, calling for valor, be propitious to us

May Bṛhaspati, the granter of wisdom, be propitious to us.

May Viṣṇu, of long strides, who is our preserver, be propitious to us.

Prayer Seeking Virtue

उरुष्या णो अभिशस्तेः सोम नि पाह्यंहसः ।
सखा सुशेव एधि नः । ।। ऋ. 1-91-15 ।।

uruṣyā ṇō abhiśastēḥ sōma ni pāhyaṃhasaḥ
sakhā suśēva ēdhi naḥ

Protect us God from the sin of slandering others. Pleased with our dedication (to virtue), become our friend.

Prayer Expressing Repentance

त्वं हि विश्वतोमुख विश्वतः परिभूरसि ।
अप नः शोशुचद् अघम् । ।। ऋ. 1-97-6 ।।

tvaṃ hi viśvatōmukha viśvataḥ paribhūrasi
apa naḥ śōśucad agham

Lord! You see it all because you are present everywhere. You notice our sins. May we be repentant of our sins.

Work Ethic and Charity

अध स्वप्नस्य निर्विदेऽभुञ्जतश् च रेवतः ।
उभा ता बस्रि नश्यतः । ।। ऋ. 1-120-12 ।।

adha svapnasya nirvidē'bhuñjataś ca rēvataḥ
ubhā tā basri naśyataḥ

God!

You are disdainful of the lazy.

You are disdainful of the rich person who does not help the poor and the needy.

They both quickly perish.

Good Actions

उदीरतां सूनृता उत् पुरन्धीर्, उद् अग्नयः शुशुचानासो अस्थुः ।
।। ऋ. 1-123-6 ।।

udīratāṃ sūnṛtā ut purandhīr, ud agnayaḥ śuśucānāsō asthuḥ

Let the words of truth be spoken.

Let the deeds of wisdom be performed.

Charity Pleases God

दक्षिणावताम् इद् इमानि चित्रा दक्षिणावतां दिवि सूर्यासः ।
दक्षिणावन्तो अमृतं भजन्ते दक्षिणावन्तः प्र तिरन्त आयुः ।।
।। ऋ. 1-125-6 ।।

dakṣiṇāvatām id imāni citrā dakṣiṇāvatāṃ divi sūryāsaḥ dakṣiṇāvantō amṛtaṃ bhajantē dakṣiṇāvantaḥ pra tiranta āyuḥ

Wonderful rewards await for those who give pious gifts. The Sun shines in heaven for such persons. They enjoy a long, happy life in this world and indeed attain immortality.

Commentary

In the Vedic scriptures immortality refers not to either the body or the soul; for the body must die. It invariably refers to the attainment of a state of mind in which a person loses the fear of death of his body.

Bless the Prayerful

मा पृणन्तो दुरितम् एन आरन् मा जारिषुः सूरयः सुव्रतासः ।
अन्यस् तेषां परिधिर् अस्तु कश्चिद् अपृणन्तम् अभि सं यन्तु शोकाः ।।
।। ऋ. 1-125-7 ।।

mā pṛṇantō duritam ēna āran mā jāriṣuḥ sūrayaḥ suvratāsaḥ
anyas tēṣāṃ paridhir astu kaścid apṛṇantam abhi saṃ yantu śōkāḥ

May those who offer prayers to God not commit heinous sin.

May those who praise God not experience decay.

May God-loving people always be helped by other people.

May afflictions fall on only those who never offer prayers.

Maligning Others

यो नो अग्ने अररिवान् अघायुर् अरातीवा मर्चयति द्वयेन ।
मन्त्रो गुरुः पुनर् अस्तु सो अस्मा अनु मृक्षीष्ट तन्वं दुरुक्तैः ।।
।। ऋ. 1-147-4 ।।

yō nō agnē ararivān aghāyur arātīvā marcayati dvayēna
mantrō guruḥ punar astu sō asmā anu mṛkṣīṣṭa tanvaṃ duruktaiḥ

A wicked person who maligns others by his speech, thinks ill of others, refrains from charity, and indulges in deceit and trickery, hurts himself by his own such deeds.

Charity

व्यनिनस्य धनिनः प्रहोषे चिद् अररुषः ।
कदा चन प्रजिगतो अदेवयोः । ॥ ऋ. 1-150-2 ॥

vyaninasya dhaninaḥ prahōṣē cid araruṣaḥ
kadā cana prajigatō adēvayōḥ

God withholds his favors from the rich person who is Godless and who is not interested in giving charity.

Good Actions

तदस्य प्रियमभि पाथो अश्यां नरो यत्र देवयवो मदन्ति ।
उरुक्रमस्य स हि बन्धुरित्था विष्णोः पदे परमे मध्व उत्सः ॥
॥ ऋ. 1-154-5 ॥

tadasya priyamabhi pāthō aśyāṃ narō yatra dēvayavō madanti
urukramasya sa hi bandhuritthā viṣṇōḥ padē paramē madhva utsaḥ

May I travel the Lord's favorite path, which is the delight of God-seeking men; and which leads me to wide stepping Viṣṇu, the friend of the pious, and whose abode is all bliss.

One God

अचिकित्वाञ्चिकितुषश् चिद् अत्र
कवीन् पृच्छामि विद्मने न विद्वान् ।
वि यस् तस्तम्भ षळिमा रजांस्यजस्य
रूपे किमपि स्विद् एकम् ।।
।। ऋ. 1-164-6 ।।

acikitvāñcikituṣaś cid atra kavīn pṛcchāmi vidmanē na vidvān
vi yas tastambha ṣaḷimā rajāṃsyajasya rūpē kimapi svid ēkam

The wise sages know; and they tell us about the One unborn Lord who upholds the universe.

Discretion in Speech

चत्वारि वाक् परिमिता पदानि तानि विदुर् ब्राह्मणा ये मनीषिणः ।
गुहा त्रीणि निहिता नेङ्गयन्ति तुरीयं वाचो मनुष्या वदन्ति ।।
।। ऋ. 1-164-45 ।।

catvāri vāk parimitā padāni tāni vidur brāhmaṇā yē manīṣiṇaḥ
guhā trīṇi nihitā nēṅgayanti turīyaṃ vācō manuṣyā vadanti

If all speech could be divided into four equal parts, the wise will replace three parts with silence.

One God

इन्द्रं मित्रं वरुणम् अग्निम् आहुर् अथो दिव्यः स सुपर्णो गरुत्मान् ।
एकं सद् विप्रा बहुधा वदन्त्यग्निं यमं मातरिश्वानम् आहुः ।।
।। ऋ. 1-164-46 ।।

indraṃ mitraṃ varuṇam agnim āhur athō divyaḥ sa suparṇō garutmān
ēkaṃ sad viprā bahudhā vadantyagniṃ yamaṃ mātariśvānam āhuḥ

There is that One God they call by so many names: Indra, Mitra, Varuṇa, Agni, Garutmat, Yama, Mātariśvan.

Unity

न मृषा श्रान्तं यद्अवन्ति देवा विश्वा इत् स्पृधो अभ्यश्नवाव ।
जयावेदत्र शतनीथम् आजिं यत् सम्यञ्चा मिथुनावभ्यजाव ।।
।। ऋ. 1-179-3 ।।

na mṛṣā śrāntaṃ yadavanti dēvā viśvā it spṛdhō abhyaśnavāva
jayāvēdatra śatanītham ājiṃ yat samyañcā mithunāvabhyajāva

Worship does not go in vain.

God is our protector. He wants us to enjoy our life. When danger faces us from outside he wants us to face it by uniting together and by so doing obtain victory.

Creation

कतरा पूर्वा कतरा परायोः कथा जाते कवयः को वि वेद ।
विश्वं त्मना बिभृतो यद्ध नाम वि वर्तेते अहनी चक्रियेव ।।
।। ऋ. 1-185-1 ।।

katarā pūrvā katarā parāyōḥ kathā jātē kavayaḥ kō vi vēda
viśvaṃ tmanā bibhṛtō yaddha nāma vi vartētē ahanī cakriyēva

How did the earth and the sky come into being? In what order were the various components of the universe created?

No one knows, not even the most learned amongst us. All we know is that the day and night keep revolving as though mounted on a wheel.

Prayer Seeking Good Life

अनेहो दात्रम् अदितेर् अनर्वं हुवे स्वर्वद् अवधं नमस्वत् ।
तद् रोदसी जनयतं जरित्रे द्यावा रक्षतं पृथिवी नो अभ्वात् ।।
।। ऋ. 1-185-3 ।।

anēhō dātram aditēr anarvaṃ huvē svarvad avadhaṃ namasvat
tad rōdasī janayataṃ jaritrē dyāvā rakṣataṃ pṛthivī nō abhvāt

Aditi! I pray to you for prosperity; for a life without injury and pain. I pray for abundance of food.

Protect us from all kinds of dangers and evil forces.

Prayer Expressing Repentance

देवान्वा यच् चकृमा कच्चिद् आगः सखायं वा सदमिज्जास्पतिं वा ।
इयं धीर् भूया अवयानम् एषां द्यावा रक्षतं पृथिवी नो अभ्वात् ।।
।। ऋ. 1-185-8 ।।

dēvānvā yac cakṛmā kaccid āgaḥ sakhāyaṃ vā sadamijjāspatiṃ vā
iyaṃ dhīr bhūyā avayānam ēṣāṃ dyāvā rakṣataṃ pṛthivī nō abhvāt

We may have committed sins against friends and family members. We repentantly pray to you for forgiveness, because these are sins against You, O Dēvas.

Charity

उभा शंसा नर्या माम् अविष्टाम् उभे माम् ऊती अवसा सचेताम् ।
भूरि चिदर्यः सुदास्तरायेषा मदन्त इषयेम देवाः ।।
।। ऋ. 1-185-9 ।।

ubhā śaṃsā naryā mām aviṣṭām ubhē mām ūtī avasā sacētām
bhūri cidaryaḥ sudāstarāyēṣā madanta iṣayēma dēvāḥ

I am desirous of prosperity for the sake of making generous gifts. May heaven and earth attend me with favor.

Prayer Seeking Wisdom and Prosperity

अग्ने नय सुपथा राये अस्मान् विश्वानि देव वयुनानि विद्वान् ।
युयोध्यस्मज् जुहुराणम् एनो भूयिष्ठां ते नमउक्तिं विधेम ।।
।। ऋ. 1-189-1 ।।

agnē naya supathā rāyē asmān viśvāni dēva vayunāni vidvān
yuyōdhyasmaj juhurāṇam ēnō bhūyiṣṭhāṃ tē namauktiṃ vidhēma

Lord! We bring to you our adoration!
Lead us through the righteous path to riches.
Lord! you know every sacred duty.
Remove the thoughts from our minds that make us stray and wander.

Maṇḍala 2

In Praise of God

यस्मान्न ऋते विजयन्ते जनासो यं युध्यमाना अवसे हवन्ते ।
यो विश्वस्य प्रतिमानं बभूव यो अच्युतच्युत् स जनास इन्द्रः ।।
।। ऋ. 2-12-9 ।।

yasmānna ṛtē vijayantē janāsō yaṃ yudhyamānā avasē havantē
yō viśvasya pratimānaṃ babhūva yō acyutacyut sa janāsa indraḥ

He, without whose blessing men do not conquer the enemy; whom when going to the battlefield we invoke; whose divine power the universe reflects; He, O men, is the Lord.

Prayer Seeking Health, Wealth, and Virtue

इन्द्र श्रेष्ठानि द्रविणानि धेहि चित्तिं दक्षस्य सुभगत्वम् अस्मे ।
पोषं रयीणाम् अरिष्टिं तनूनां स्वाद्मानं वाचः सुदिनत्वम् अह्नाम् ।।
।। ऋ. 2-21-6 ।।

indra śrēṣṭhāni draviṇāni dhēhi cittiṃ dakṣasya subhagatvam asmē
pōṣaṃ rayiṇām ariṣṭiṃ tanūnāṃ svādmānaṃ vācaḥ sudinatvam ahnām

O God!
Bestow on us bounteous wealth;
Bless us with good minds;
Give us healthy bodies, sweet speech, and fair days.

Prayer of Devotion

गणानां त्वा गणपतिꣳ हवामहे कविं कवीनाम् उपमश्रवस् तमम् ।
ज्येष्ठ राजं ब्रह्मणां ब्रह्मणस्पत आ नः शृण्वन्नूतिभिः सीद सादनम् ।।
।। ऋ. 2-23-1 ।।

gaṇānāṃ tvā gaṇapatiṃ havāmahē
kaviṃ kavīnām upamaśravas tamam
jyēṣṭha rājaṃ brahmaṇāṃ brahmaṇaspata
ā naḥ śṛṇvannūtibhiḥ sīda sādanam

O God! O Gaṇapati
Among us, your subjects, You are our master. Hail to you.
Among those who are wise, You are the wisest.
Among superiors, You are the highest lord.
Among the glorious, You are the most glorious.
Among the souls, You are the Supreme Soul.
With this prayer, Lord, we are asking You to bless us with your presence in our midst to give us Your protection.

Commentary

This is the first prayer composed in the Vēdas, addressing God as Gaṇapati. The second prayer is mantra 23-19 of Yajurvēda (Vājasanēyī) Saṃhitā. During Vēdic times Gaṇapati was an epithet of a formless God. Later Gaṇapati or Gaṇeśa was given a form and also parents.

Prayer Seeking Virtue

बृहस्पते अति यद्अर्यो अर्हाद् द्युमद् विभाति क्रतुमज् जनेषु ।
यद् दीदयच् छवस ऋतप्रजात तदस्मासु द्रविणं धेहि चित्रम् ।।
।। ऋ. 2-23-15 ।।

bṛhaspatē ati yadaryō arhād dyumad vibhāti kratumaj janēṣu
yad dīdayac chavasa ṛtaprajāta tadasmāsu draviṇaṃ dhēhi citram

O kind Lord!
May we earn wealth and glory by right means. May our wealth help others achieve glory.

God, Make Me Virtuous

माहं मघोनो वरुण प्रियस्य भूरिदाव्न आ विदं शूनमापेः ।
मा रायो राजन्त्सुयमादव स्थां बृहद् वदेम विदथे सुवीराः ।।
।। ऋ. 2-27-17 ।।

māhaṃ maghōnō varuṇa priyasya bhūridāvna ā vidaṃ śūnamāpēḥ
mā rāyō rājantsuyamādava sthāṃ bṛhad vadēma vidathē suvīrāḥ

O God! May I never bad-mouth the persons who are rich but charitable, who perform virtuous deeds, and who are elders and worthy of respect. May wealth not make me arrogant; may you grant me virtuous children; and may I never fail to be worshipful to you.

God's Generosity

त्वादत्तेभी रुद्र शं तमेभिः शतं हिमा अशीय भेषजेभिः ।
व्यस्मद् द्वेषो वितरं व्यंहो व्यमीवाश् चातयस्वा विषूचीः ।।
।। ऋ. 2-33-2 ।।

tvādattēbhī rudra śaṃ tamēbhiḥ śataṃ himā aśīya bhēṣajēbhiḥ
vyasmad dvēṣō vitaraṃ vyaṃhō vyamīvāś cātayasvā viṣūcīḥ

O God!

You have blessed us with so many medicinal plants. With the help of the cures you have provided, may I sustain myself well, so that I could keep busy in productive work for a life span of hundred years. Not only may I keep sickness out of my body, I should also remove sinful thoughts from my mind, and in particular ill-will against any fellow man.

Maṇḍala 3

Prosperity, Power, and Wisdom

आ भारती भारतीभिः सजोषा इळा देवैर् मनुष्येभिर् अग्निः ।
सरस्वती सारस्वतेभिर् अर्वाक् तिस्रो देवीर् बर्हिरेदं सदन्तु ।।
।। ऋ. 3-4-8 ।।

ā bhāratī bhāratībhiḥ sajōṣā iḷā dēvair manuṣyēbhir agniḥ
sarasvatī sārasvatēbhir arvāk tisrō dēvīr barhirēdaṃ sadantu

Let the three Goddesses - Bhāratī, the Goddess of prosperity, Iḷā, the Goddess of power, and Sarasvatī, the Goddess of wisdom, come and sit down amidst us.

One God

विश्वेदेते जनिमा सं विविक्तो महो देवान् बिभ्रती न व्यथेते ।
एजद् ध्रुवं पत्यते विश्वम्एकं चरत् पतत्रि विषुणं वि जातम् ।।
।। ऋ. 3-54-8 ।।

viśvēdētē janimā saṃ viviktō mahō dēvān bibhratī na vyathētē
ējad dhruvaṃ patyatē viśvamēkaṃ carat patatri viṣuṇaṃ vi jātam

(The heaven holds in its bosom the planets, the stars, the sun, and the moon, just as the earth holds the living beings and non-living things.) The heaven and the earth grant to everyone born a distinct identity; yet all life, moving and stationary, depends on One Supreme Being.

God's Laws

न ता मिनन्ति मायिनो न धीरा व्रता देवानां प्रथमा ध्रुवाणि ।
न रोदसी अद्रुहा वेद्याभिर् न पर्वता निनमे तस्थिवांसः ।।
।। ऋ. 3-56-1 ।।

na tā minanti māyinō na dhīrā vratā dēvānāṃ prathamā dhruvāṇi
na rōdasī adruhā vēdyābhir na parvatā ninamē tasthivāṃsaḥ

God's laws are excellent and eternal. No one can break or disobey them – neither the conniving enemies of men nor the wisest among us. Not even the earth or the heaven can challenge them. They are like mountains which never bend.

Service of Others

या ते अग्ने पर्‌वतस्येव धारासश्चन्ती पीपयद्‌ देव चित्रा ।
ताम्‌ अस्मभ्यं प्रमतिं जातवेदो वसो रास्व सुमतिं विश्वजन्याम्‌ ।।
।। ऋ. 3-57-6 ।।

yā tē agnē parvatasyēva dhārāsaścantī pīpayad dēva citrā
tām asmabhyaṃ pramatiṃ jātavēdō vasō rāsva sumatiṃ viśvajanyām

O Divine Agni! Your generosity is like that of the stream of water that flows down the mountain slopes to provide comfort to the parched earth. We ask you to instill in us the same magnanimity as you have, so that we get busy benefitting others.

Prayer Seeking Wisdom

(ॐ भूर्‌ भुवः स्वः)
तत्‌ सवितुर्‌ वरेण्यं भर्‌गो देवस्य धीमहि ।
धियो यो नः प्रचोदयात्‌ । ।। ऋ. 3-62-10 ।।

(Ōṃ bhūr bhuvaḥ svaḥ)
tat savitur varēṇyaṃ bhargō dēvasya dhīmahi
dhiyō yō naḥ pracōdayāt

Gāyatrī Mantra

(i) (The Earth, the Sky, and the Heaven praise Him.) Let us meditate on the glory of the divine Lord. He is the One who sustains us. We pray to Him that He may direct our understanding by instilling wisdom in us.

Commentary

This is the most famous of all Vedic mantras, and is called Gāyatrī mantra after the meter in which it is composed. "Ōṃ bhūr, bhuvaḥ, svaḥ" are not part of the mantra. Ōṃ is always put at the beginning of a mantra, or a set of mantras. "bhūr, bhuvaḥ, svaḥ" — the set of three words, is called vyāhṛti. It is always prefixed to this mantra and also to many other mantras.

Maṇḍala 4

Prayer Seeking Mercy

त्राता नो बोधि ददृशान आपिर् अभिख्याता मर्डिता सोम्यानाम् ।
सखा पिता पितृतमः पितॄणां, कर्तेमु लोकम् उशते वयोधाः ।।
।। ऋ. 4-17-17 ।।

trātā nō bōdhi dadṛśāna āpir abhikhyātā marḍitā sōmyānām
sakhā pitā pitṛtamaḥ pitṝṇāṃ, kartēmu lōkam uśatē vayōdhāḥ

Lord! Be our preserver. Look after us and be merciful to us, your worshippers. You are the friend and the most loving father, giving to us land and food.

Work Ethic

इदाह्नः पीतिम् उत वो मदं धुर् न ऋते श्रान्तस्य सख्याय देवाः ।
।। ऋ. 4-33-11 ।।

idāhnaḥ pītim uta vō madaṃ dhur na ṛtē śrāntasya sakhyāya dēvāḥ

Men! God has given you the elixir of life. Yet, He is a friend of only those who work hard.

Omnipresence of God

हंसः शुचिषद् वसुर् अन्तरिक्षसद्,
होता वेदिषद् अतिथिर् दुरोणसत् ।
नृषद् वरसद् ऋतसद् व्योमसद्
अब्जा गोजा ऋतजा अद्रिजा ऋतम् ।।
।। ऋ. 4-40-5 ।।

haṃsaḥ śuciṣad vasur antarikṣasad,
hōtā vēdiṣad atithir durōṇasat
nṛṣad varasad ṛtasad vyōmasad
abjā gōjā ṛtajā adrijā ṛtam

The most glorious Lord is in the clouds, the sky, the heaven, and everywhere else. Recognize him in the guest visiting with you. He is present in all men and in greater measure in the body of the priest and virtuous men. He is reachable through worship and through the path of truth and virtue.

Commentary

This mantra is of great significance for two reasons: 1) it contains the seed of what blossomed in the Upaniṣads - the statement that God resides in the body of human beings; and 2) it justifies calling a great and virtuous person "mahātmā" (the great soul).

Prayer Seeking Happiness

बृहत् सुम्नः प्रसवीता निवेशनो जगतः स्थातुर् उभयस्य यो वशी ।
स नो देवः सविता शर्म यच्छत्वस्मे क्षयाय त्रिवरुथम् अंहसः ।।
।। ऋ. 4-53-6 ।।

bṛhat sumnaḥ prasavītā nivēśanō jagataḥ sthātur ubhayasya yō vaśī
sa nō dēvaḥ savitā śarma yacchatvasmē kṣayāya trivarutham aṃhasaḥ

O most gracious Lord! You bring the world to life and you maintain its stability. You control the animate and the inanimate. Grant us freedom from three types of sin — sins of improper thinking, improper speech, and improper action.

Prayer Seeking Forgiveness

अचित्ती यच्चकृमा दैव्ये जने दीनैर् दक्षैः प्रभूती पूरुषत्वता ।
देवेषु च सवितर् मानुषेषु च त्वं नो अत्र सुवताद् अनागसः ।।
।। ऋ. 4-54-3 ।।

acittī yaccakṛmā daivyē janē dīnair dakṣaiḥ prabhūtī pūruṣatvatā
dēvēṣu ca savitar mānuṣēṣu ca tvaṃ nō atra suvatād anāgasaḥ

God! If through ignorance, through unmindfulness, through conceit, or through human weaknesses we have committed offense against you or against men, we pray to you to pardon us.

Maṇḍala 5

Prayer Seeking Virtue

अस्माकम् अग्ने अध्वरं जुषस्व सहसः सूनो त्रिषधस्थ हव्यम् ।
वयं देवेषु सुकृतः स्याम शर्मणा नस् त्रिवरूथेन पाहि ॥
॥ ऋ. 5-4-8 ॥

asmākam agnē adhvaraṃ juṣasva sahasaḥ sūnō triṣadhastha havyam
vayaṃ dēvēṣu sukṛtaḥ syāma śarmaṇā nas trivarūthēna pāhi

Accept, O Dēvas, our oblations and prayers. Grant us that we may be good in three ways: (1) in thought, (2) in speech, and (3) in action.

Prayer Seeking Glory and Immortality

यस्त्वा हृदा कीरिणा मन्यमानोऽमर्त्यं मर्त्यो जोहवीमि ।
जातवेदो यशो अस्मासु धेहि प्रजाभिरग्ने अमृतत्वम् अश्याम् ॥
॥ ऋ. 5-4-10 ॥

yastvā hṛdā kīriṇā manyamānō'martyaṃ martyō jōhavīmi
jātavēdō yaśō asmāsu dhēhi prajābhiragnē amṛtatvam aśyām

I am a mortal and your are eternal, O God! I praise you with devotion, and ask you two favors: (1) That we may earn glory, and (2) That we may gain immortality through an unbroken line of descendants.

Prayer Seeking the Welfare of Friends

तं त्वा शोचिष्ठ दीदिवः सुम्नाय नूनम् ईमहे सखिभ्यः ।
स नो बोधि श्रुधी हवम् उरुष्या णो अघायतः समस्मात् ।।
।। ऋ. 5-24-4 & 3 ।।

taṃ tvā śōciṣṭha dīdivaḥ sumnāya nūnam īmahē sakhibhyaḥ
sa nō bōdhi śrudhī havam uruṣyā ṇō aghāyataḥ samasmāt

To you O glorious One, we come to pray for the welfare of our friends. Listen to our prayers and keep evil men away from them.

Prayer Seeking Reward for Virtue

तवोतिभिः सचमाना अरिष्टा बृहस्पते मघवानः सुवीराः ।
ये अश्वदा उत वा सन्ति गोदा ये वस्त्रदाः सुभगास् तेषु रायः ।।
।। ऋ. 5-42-8 ।।

tavōtibhiḥ sacamānā ariṣṭā bṛhaspatē maghavānaḥ suvīrāḥ
yē aśvadā uta vā santi gōdā yē vastradāḥ subhagās tēṣu rāyaḥ

O Lord! Because of your grace men live unharmed, are blessed with children, and become wealthy. May your generosity go to those who are generous in giving horses, cows, and clothing (to those in need).

Virtue and Prayer

यो जागार तम् ऋचः कामयन्ते यो जागार तमु सामानि यन्ति ।
यो जागार तम् अयं सोम आह तवाहम् अस्मि सख्ये न्योकाः ।।
।। ऋ. 5-44-14 ।।

yō jāgāra tam ṛcaḥ kāmayantē yō jāgāra tamu sāmāni yanti
yō jāgāra tam ayaṃ sōma āha tavāham asmi sakhyē nyōkāḥ

The ṛcās of the Ṛgvēda Saṃhitā and the Sāmas of the Sāmavēda Saṃhitā are prayer-mantras of the scripture. They benefit the one who is awake (to his duties). To him God whispers, "I am yours, and I will remain your friend".

Prayer Seeking Welfare

स्वस्ति नो मिमीताम् अश्विना भगः स्वस्ति देव्यदितिर् अनर्वणः ।
स्वस्ति पूषा असुरो दधातु नः स्वस्ति द्यावा पृथिवी सुचेतुना ।।
।। ऋ. 5-51-11 ।।

स्वस्तये वायुम् उप ब्रवामहै सोमं स्वस्ति भुवनस्य यस्पतिः ।
बृहस्पतिं सर्वगणं स्वस्तये स्वस्तय आदित्यासो भवन्तु नः ।।
।। ऋ. 5-51-12 ।।

स्वस्ति मित्रा वरुणा स्वस्ति पथ्ये रेवति ।
स्वस्ति न इन्द्रश्चाग्निश् च स्वस्ति नो आदिते कृधि ।।
।। ऋ. 5-51-14 ।।

svasti nō mimītām aśvinā bhagaḥ svasti dēvyaditir anarvaṇaḥ
svasti pūṣā asurō dadhātu naḥ svasti dyāvā pṛthivī sucētunā

svastayē vāyum upa bravāmahai sōmaṃ svasti bhuvanasya yaspatiḥ
bṛhaspatiṃ sarvagaṇaṃ svastayē svastaya ādityāsō bhavantu naḥ

svasti mitrā varuṇā svasti pathyē rēvati
svasti na indraścāgniś ca svasti nō āditē kṛdhi

Lord, we seek your blessings.
May you as Aśvins bless us;
May you as Bhaga bless us;
May you as Aditi bless us;
May you as Pūṣan bless us;
May you as Heaven and Earth bless us;
May you as Vāyu bless us;
May you as Sōma bless us;

May you as Bṛhaspati bless us;
May you as Āditya bless us;
May you as Mitra bless us;
May you as Varuṇa bless us;
May you as Indra bless us;
May you as Agni bless us;

Prayer Seeking Welfare

स्वस्ति - वचन

विश्वे देवा नो अद्या स्वस्तये वैश्वानरो वसुरग्निः स्वस्तये ।
देवा अवन्त्वृभवः स्वस्तये स्वस्ति नो रुद्रः पात्वंहसः ।।
।। ऋ. 5-51-13 ।।

viśvē dēvā nō adyā svastayē vaiśvānarō vasuragniḥ svastayē
dēvā avantvṛbhavaḥ svastayē svasti nō rudraḥ pātvaṃhasaḥ

With the worship of fire, we ask all the Dēvas to come to our home today. We welcome you to our home so that you may help us get rid of all our troubles and evil ways.

Promise of Virtue

स्वस्ति पन्थाम् अनुचरेम सूर्याचन्द्रमसाविव ।
पुनर् ददताघ्नता जानता सं गमेमहि । ।। ऋ. 5-51-15 ।।

svasti panthām anucarēma sūryācandramasāviva
punar dadatāghnatā jānatā saṃ gamēmahi

We shall follow the virtuous path steadfastly like the sun and the moon follow their paths. We shall associate with the generous, the kind, and the learned.

Prayer Seeking Virtue

विश्वानि देव सवितर् दुरितानि परा सुव ।
यद् भद्रं तन्न आ सुव । ।। ऋ. 5-82-5 ।।

viśvāni dēva savitar duritāni parā suva
yad bhadraṃ tanna ā suva

O God! the lord of the universe! the stimulator of good thoughts! We ask you to steer us away from an evil path. Please put us on a course which has your blessings.

Prayer Seeking Virtue

अर्‌यम्यं वरुण मित्र्यं वा सखायं वा सदम् इद् भ्रातरं वा ।
वेशं वा नित्यं वरुणारणं वा यत् सीमागश् चकृमा शिश्रथस् तत् ।।
।। ऋ. 5-85-7 ।।

aryamyaṃ varuṇa mitryaṃ vā sakhāyaṃ vā sadam id bhrātaraṃ vā
vēśaṃ vā nityaṃ varuṇāraṇaṃ vā yat sīmāgaś cakṛmā śiśrathas tat

O God! Forgive me if I have ever committed sin against a benefactor, a dear friend, a companion, my brother, my neighbor, or a stranger.

Commentary

This is not only a prayer for forgiveness, it is a promise not to commit sin against anyone, not even strangers.

Repentance for Sin

कितवासो यद् रिरिपुर् न दीवि यद् वा घा सत्यम् उत यन् न विद्म ।
सर्वा ता वि ष्य शिथिरेव देवाधा ते स्याम वरुण प्रियासः ।।
।। ऋ. 5-85-8 ।।

kitavāsō yad riripur na dīvi yad vā ghā satyam uta yan na vidma
sarvā tā vi ṣya śithirēva dēvādhā tē syāma varuṇa priyāsaḥ

O God! We may have committed the sin of blaming others in error just like gamblers do when they argue; we may have knowingly committed sin; or we may have unknowingly performed evil deeds. We pray to you to rid us of all three kinds of sin so that we remain your beloved.

Maṇḍala 6

Prayer of Devotion

वि मे करणा पतयतो वि चक्षुर् वीउदं ज्योतिर् हृदय आहितं यत् ।
वि मे मनश्चरति दूर आधीः किं स्विद् वक्ष्यामि किमु नू मनिष्ये ।।
।। ऋ. 6-9-6 ।।

vi mē karṇā patayatō vi cakṣur vīdaṃ jyōtir hṛdaya āhitaṃ yat
vi mē manaścarati dūra ādhīḥ kiṃ svid vakṣyāmi kimu nū maniṣyē

Lord! How do I comprehend you?
Let my ears be turned to hear you;
Let my eyes be opened to behold you;
Let my mind be eager to know you;
Let my heart be absorbed in you.
What more shall I say?

Agni

अग्न आ याहि वीतये गृणानो हव्यदातये ।
नि होता सत्सि बर्हिषि । ।। ऋ. 6-16-10 ।।

agna ā yāhi vītayē gṛṇānō havyadātayē
ni hōtā satsi barhiṣi

O Agni! Come and take your seat amidst us; hear the praise, and accept the oblations of foodgrains from us. Bless us with plenty of food.

Charity

क्रत्वा दा अस्तु श्रेष्ठोऽद्य त्वा वन्वन्त् सुरेक्णाः ।
मर्त आनाश सुवृक्तिम् । ।। ऋ. 6-16-26 ।।

kratvā dā astu śrēṣṭhō'dya tvā vanvant surēkṇāḥ
marta ānāśa suvṛktim

Lord, Give power to his speech and grant him prosperity who serves you through his noble actions and charity.

Prayer Seeking Courage and Motivation

उरुं नो लोकम् अनुनेषि विद्वान्त् स्वर्वज् ज्योतिर् अभयं स्वस्ति ।
ऋष्वा त इन्द्र स्थविरस्य बाहू उपस्थेयाम शरणा बृहन्ता ॥
॥ ऋ. 6-47-8 ॥

urum nō lōkam anunēṣi vidvānt svarvaj jyōtir abhayam svasti
ṛṣvā ta indra sthavirasya bāhū upasthēyāma śaraṇā bṛhantā

In this wide world O Lord, we need your continuous guidance. You are the heavenly beacon of light with infinite wisdom. Bless us to becoming fearless and highly motivated. We surrender ourselves O Lord, into your strong arms.

Prayer Seeking Welfare

त्रातारम् इन्द्रम् अवितारम् इन्द्रं हवेहवे सुहवं शूरम् इन्द्रम् ।
ह्वयामि शक्रं पुरुहूतम् इन्द्रं स्वस्ति नो मघवा धात्विन्द्रः ॥
॥ ऋ. 6-47-11 ॥

trātāram indram avitāram indram havēhavē suhavam śūram indram
hvayāmi śakram puruhūtam indram svasti nō maghavā dhātvindraḥ

The Lord is the savior, the protector, and the almighty whom we joyfully invoke. May He, the magnanimous, confer His blessing on us.

Charity

अदित् सन्तं चिद् आघृणे पूषन् दानाय चोदय ।
पणेश् चिद् वि म्रदा मनः । || ऋ. 6-53-3 ||

adit santaṃ cid āghṛṇē pūṣan dānāya cōdaya
paṇēś cid vi mradā manaḥ

Glorious Lord! Instigate the niggard to become generous and charitable; soften the heart of the miser.

Prayer Seeking Wisdom

सं पूषन् विदुषा नय यो अञ्जसानुशासति ।
य एवेदम् इति ब्रवत् । || ऋ. 6-54-1 ||

saṃ pūṣan viduṣā naya yō añjasānuśāsati
ya ēvēdam iti bravat

Bring us, O Lord, in touch with a wise person who may rightly direct us; who may say, "This is the way".

Maṇḍala 7

Prayer for God's Mercy

शं नो धाता शम् उ धर्ता नो अस्तु शं न उरूची भवतु स्वधाभिः ।
शं रोदसी बृहती शं नो अद्रिः शं नो देवानां सुहवानि सन्तु ।।
।। ऋ. 7-35-3 ।।

śaṃ nō dhātā śam u dhartā nō astu śaṃ na urūcī bhavatu svadhābhiḥ
śaṃ rōdasī bṛhatī śaṃ nō adriḥ śaṃ nō dēvānāṃ suhavāni santu

May the Dēvas be beneficent to us. May the Dēvas, our sustainers, be beneficent to us. May the Dēvas be beneficent to us willingly and generously. May heaven and earth be beneficient to us. May our prayers bring us beneficent response.

Commentary

This mantra is often used as a prayer. The Saṃskṛta word śam may mean welfare, beneficence, or favorable inclination. The two most popular compound words from śam are Śaṅkara and Śambhu, both meaning "God, who looks after our welfare". Some lexicons have translated śam as peace but more often it denotes welfare.

Prayer Seeking Progeny

ये देवानां यज्ञिया यज्ञियानां मनोर्यजत्रा अमृता ऋतज्ञाः ।
ते नो रासन्ताम् उरुगायम् अद्य यूयं पात स्वस्तिभिः सदा नः ।।
।। ऋ. 7-35-15 ।।

yē dēvānāṃ yajñiyā yajñiyānāṃ manōryajatrā amṛtā ṛtajñāḥ
tē nō rāsantām urugāyam adya yūyaṃ pāta svastibhiḥ sadā naḥ

The most respectable, the imperishable and the most righteous Dēvas were prayed by Manu, the progenitor.

Today we pray to them to bless us with a child who will grow up and attain glory. May we be blessed by you O Lord.

Prayer of Devotion

अस्य देवस्य मीळ्हुषो वया विष्णोर् एषस्य प्रभृथे हविर्भिः ।
विदे हि रुद्रो रुद्रियं महित्वं यासिष्टं वर्तिरश्विनाविरावत् ।।
।। ऋ. 7-40-5 ।।

asya dēvasya mīḷahuṣō vayā viṣṇōr ēṣasya prabhṛthē havirbhiḥ
vidē hi rudrō rudriyaṃ mahitvaṃ yāsiṣṭaṃ vartiraśivanāvirāvat

I offer my prayers and oblations to divine Viṣṇu and beneficent Rudra. I pray to the Aśvins to come to my dwelling.

House-Warming Prayers

वास्तोष्पते प्रति जानीह्यस्मान्त् स्वावेशो अनमीवो भवा नः ।
यत् त्वेमहे प्रति तन्नो जुषस्व शं नो भव द्विपदे शं चतुष्पदे ।।
।। ऋ. 7-54-1 ।।

vāstōṣpatē prati jānīhyasmānt svāvēśō anamīvō bhavā naḥ
yat tvēmahē prati tannō juṣasva śaṃ nō bhava dvipadē śaṃ catuṣpadē

O Lord of this dwelling!

Recognize us. Let this house bring us comfort. Protect us from ill health. Be pleased to fulfill our dreams. Bestow your blessings upon us and on our animals.

वास्तोष्पते प्रतरणो न एधि गयस्फानो गोभिर् अश्वेभिर् इन्दो ।
अजरासस् ते सख्ये स्याम पितेव पुत्रान् प्रति नो जुषस्व ।।
।। ऋ. 7-54-2 ।।

vāstōṣpatē prataraṇō na ēdhi gayasphānō gōbhir aśvēbhir indō
ajarāsas tē sakhyē syāma pitēva putrān prati nō juṣasva

O Lord of this dwelling!

Be our protector and preserver. Augment our wealth. May we, through your friendship, become exempt from decay. Be caring to us like a father is to his children.

वास्तोष्पते शग्मया संसदा ते सक्षीमहि रण्वया गातुमत्या ।
पाहि क्षेम उत योगे वरं नो यूयं पात स्वस्तिभिः सदा नः ।।
।। ऋ. 7-54-3 ।।

vāstōṣpatē śagmayā saṃsadā tē sakṣīmahi raṇvayā gātumatyā
pāhi kṣēma uta yōgē varaṃ nō yūyaṃ pāta svastibhiḥ sadā naḥ

O Lord of this dwelling!

May we be possessed of a comfortable, delightful, opulent abode, granted by you. Protect our wealth whether in our possession or yet to come. Cherish us forever with your blessings.

Prayer for Sparing Life - Mṛtyuñjaya Mantra

त्र्यम्बकं यजामहे सुगन्धिं पुष्टिवर्धनम् ।
उर्वारुकम् इव बन्धनान् मृत्योर् मुक्षीय मामृतात् ।।
।। ऋ. 7-59-12 ।।

tryambakaṃ yajāmahē sugandhiṃ puṣṭivardhanam
urvārukam iva bandhanān mṛtyōr mukṣīya māmṛtāt

O Lord! The fragrance of Your glory is a source of strength to me. My breath is attached to my body just like a cucumber is attached to the cucumber plant. I pray to you – do not separate my breath from my body. Protect me from death. Grant me immortality.

Commentary

In the times of Ṛgvēda the word tryambaka, perhaps, referred to three Goddesses - Bhāratī, Iḷā, and Sarasvatī, being called the three mothers. Later on Tryambaka began to be used for Śiva, the three-eyed lord. The words "urvārukam iva bandhanān mṛtyor mukṣīya" have been translated by some as - "as cucumber separates from its plant so God you separate us from death". This translation, though literal, does not seem proper because cucumbers separate from the cucumber plant when they ripen, and so should the breath separate from the body when the body gets old. It is, therefore, better to interpret these words as though the prayer is asking God not to separate the breath from the body.

उत स्वया तन्वा सं वदे तत् कदान्वन्तर् वरुणे भुवानि ।
किं मे हव्यम् अहृणानो जुषेत कदा मृळीकं सुमना अभिख्यम् ।।
।। ऋ. 7-86-2 ।।

uta svayā tanvā saṃ vadē tat kadānvantar varuṇē bhuvāni
kiṃ mē havyam ahṛṇānō juṣēta kadā mṛḷīkaṃ sumanā abhikhyam

Would I be able to establish communion with the Lord (Varuṇa)?
Would I be able to reach Him?
Would He accept my offerings with pleasure?
When with a happy heart will I be able to receive His mercy?

Commentary

This mantra is significant because, perhaps, it is the very first written piece of devotional poem in the Hindū scripture.

The Sinner

न स स्वो दक्षो वरुण ध्रुतिः सा सुरा मन्युर् विभीदको अचित्तिः ।
अस्ति ज्यायान् कनीयस उपारे स्वप्नश् च नेदनृतस्य प्रयोता ।।
।। ऋ. 7-86-6 ।।

na sa svō dakṣō varuṇa dhrutiḥ sā surā manyur vibhīdakō acittiḥ
asti jyāyān kanīyasa upārē svapnaś ca nēdanṛtasya prayōtā

Lord! I am not in control of myself and that is the reason I have been a sinner. Alcohol, anger, gambling, and ignorance have led me into the wrong path. Even in dreams am I not free of sin.

Sin

यो मृळयाति चक्रुषे चिदागो वयं स्याम वरुणे अनागाः ।।
।। ऋ. 7-87-7 ।।

yō mṛḷayāti cakruṣē cidāgō vayaṃ syāma varuṇē anāgāḥ

May we not commit sin against the Lord who has compassion even for those who commit sin.

Prayer Seeking Virtue

क्रत्वः समह दीनता प्रतीपं जगमा शुचे ।
मृळा सुक्षत्र मृळय । || ऋ. 7-89-3 ||

kratvaḥ samaha dīnatā pratīpaṃ jagamā śucē
mṛḷā sukṣatra mṛḷaya

If because of being dull-witted I have travelled the unrighteous path, please have mercy on me, O Lord. Put me on the right path.

God's Generosity

वि चक्रमे पृथिवीम् एष एतां क्षेत्राय विष्णुर् मनुषे दशस्यन् ।
ध्रुवासो अस्य कीरयो जनास उरुक्षितिं सुजनिमा चकार ||
|| ऋ. 7-100-4 ||

vi cakramē pṛthivīm ēṣa ētāṃ kṣētrāya viṣṇur manuṣē daśasyan
dhruvāsō asya kīrayō janāsa urukṣitiṃ sujanimā cakāra

God created this earth to give it to mankind for a home. The generous Lord has created a big wide world for the human race.

Maṇḍala 8

God's Will

यथा वशन्ति देवास् तथेद् असत् तदेषां नकिरा मिनत् ।
अरावा चन मर्त्यः । || ऋ. 8-28-4 ||

yathā vaśanti dēvās tathēd asat tadēṣāṃ nakirā minat
arāvā cana martyaḥ

Whatever God desires, that assuredly comes to pass. No man can change God's will.

Prayer Seeking Progeny and Prosperity

पुत्रिणा ता कुमारिणा विश्वम् आयुर् व्यश्नुतः ।
उभा हिरण्यपेशसा । || ऋ. 8-31-8 ||

putriṇā tā kumāriṇā viśvam āyur vyaśnutaḥ
ubhā hiraṇyapēśasā

May the prayerful couples be blessed with sons and daughters, and may such couples enjoy their full span of life in prosperity, decked with gold.

God's Generosily

न किरस्य शचीनां नियन्ता सूनृतानाम् ।
न किर्वक्ता न दादिति । ।। ऋ. 8-32-15 ।।

na kirasya śacīnāṃ niyantā sūnṛtānām
na kirvaktā na dāditi

Lord! No one can point to the limits of your glorious deeds! No one can assert that you are not generous in giving.

Prayer Seeking Wisdom

इमां धियं शिक्षमाणस्य देव क्रतुं दक्षं वरुण सं शिशाधि ।।
।। ऋ. 8-42-3 ।।

imāṃ dhiyaṃ śikṣamāṇasya dēva kratuṃ dakṣaṃ varuṇa saṃ śiśādhi

O Omnipresent Lord! Sharpen my intellect, increase my wisdom, and make me a hard worker so that I may cross over all of life's difficulties.

Idle Talk and Laziness

त्रातारो देवा अधि वोचता नो मा नो निद्रा ईशत मोत जल्पिः ।।
।। ऋ. 8-48-14 ।।

trātārō dēvā adhi vōcatā nō mā nō nidrā iśata mōta jalpiḥ

O Protecter Dēvas! Let not slumber or idle talk, critical of others, overtake us.

One God

एक एवाग्निर् बहुधा समिद्ध एकः सूर्यो विश्वमनु प्रभूतः ।
एकैवोषाः सर्वमिदं विभात्येकं वा इदं वि बभूव सर्वम् ।।
।। ऋ. 8-58-2 ।।

ēka ēvāgnir bahudhā samiddha ēkaḥ sūryō viśvamanu prabhūtaḥ
ēkaivōṣāḥ sarvamidaṃ vibhātyēkaṃ vā idaṃ vi babhūva sarvam

One is Agni (fire) kindled in various ways;
One is Sūrya (sun) shining over all;
One is Uṣas (dawn) illuminating all things;
that One has become this all.

Prayer Singing Glory

अभ्यूर्णोति यन् नग्नं भिषक्ति विश्वं यत् तुरम् ।
प्रेमन्धः ख्यन्निः श्रोणो भूत् । ।। ऋ. 8-79-2 ।।

abhyūrṇōti yan nagnaṃ bhiṣakti viśvaṃ yat turam
prēmandhaḥ khyanniḥ śrōṇō bhūt

God!
You clothe the naked;
You heal the sick;
You can make the blind see; and
You can make the cripple walk.

Prayer Singing Glory

मन्ये त्वा यज्ञियं यज्ञियानां मन्ये त्वा च्यवनम् अच्युतानाम् ।
मन्ये त्वा सत्वनाम् इन्द्र केतुं मन्ये त्वा वृषभं चर्षणीनाम् ।।
।। ऋ. 8-96-4 ।।

manyē tvā yajñiyaṃ yajñiyānāṃ manyē tvā cyavanam acyutānām
manyē tvā satvanām indra kētuṃ manyē tvā vṛṣabhaṃ carṣaṇīnām

I trust you Lord! to be holier than the holiest;
I trust you Lord! to be the mover of the immovable;
I trust you Lord! to be stronger than the strongest;
I trust you Lord! to be wiser than the wisest.

Prayer Seeking Welfare

त्वं हि नः पिता वसो त्वं माता शतक्रतो बभूविथ ।
अधा ते सुम्नम् ईमहे । || ऋ. 8-98-11 ||

tvaṃ hi naḥ pitā vasō tvaṃ mātā śatakratō babhūvitha
adhā tē sumnam īmahē

O Generous Lord Indra! You are the father, and you are the mother. We pray for your blessing.

Maṇḍala 9

Virtue of Hard Work

पवित्रं ते विततं ब्रह्मणस्पते प्रभुर् गात्राणि पर्येषि विश्वतः ।
अतप्ततनूर् न तद् आमो अश्नुते श्रृतास इद् वहन्तस् तत् समाशत ।।
।। ऋ. 9-83-1 ।।

pavitraṃ tē vitataṃ brahmaṇaspatē prabhur gātrāṇi paryēṣi viśvataḥ
ataptatanūr na tad āmō aśnutē śṛtāsa id vahantas tat samāśata

Those who are kilned in the fire of hard work, gain maturity and receive your blessings, O Omniscient and Omnipresent Lord. Those immature people who live in sloth do not receive your blessing.

Prayer Seeking Good Life

यत्रानन्दाश्च मोदाश्च मुदः प्रमुद आसते ।
कामस्य यत्राप्ताः कामास् तत्र माम् अमृतं कृधीन्द्रायेन्दो परिस्रव ।।
।। ऋ. 9-113-11 ।।

yatrānandāśca mōdāśca mudaḥ pramuda āsatē
kāmasya yatrāptāḥ kāmās tatra mām amṛtaṃ kṛdhīndrāyēndō parisrava

Lord, make me immortal in a world in which my desires are fulfilled and where happiness and joy dwell.

Maṇḍala 10

Prayer for God's Mercy

आपो हि ष्ठा मयोभुवस् ता न ऊर्जे दधातन ।
महे रणाय चक्षसे । || ऋ. 10-9-1 ||

āpō hi ṣṭhā mayōbhuvas tā na ūrjē dadhātana
mahē raṇāya cakṣasē

O Lord! You are present in the life-giving water in the plants that provide our food. We pray that you make plenty of water available to us so that we could grow nourishing food, live in abundance, and have joyous life.

यो वः शिवतमो रसस् तस्य भाजयतेह नः ।
उशतीर् इव मातरः । || ऋ. 10-9-2 ||

yō vaḥ śivatamō rasas tasya bhājayatēha naḥ
uśatīr iva mātaraḥ

The clean, healthy, and tasteful water is as beneficial as a mother's milk is to the infant. May this water keep nourishing us.

Blessing

तस्मा अरं गमाम वो यस्य क्षयाय जिन्वथ ।
आपो जनयथा च नः । ।। ऋ. 10-9-3 ।।

tasmā araṃ gamāma vō yasya kṣayāya jinvatha
āpō janayathā ca naḥ

O God! We welcome your help for the destruction of our maladies. We invoke you to bless us with children and grand children.

Prayer Expressing Thankfulness

Śaṃ nō dēvī mantra शं नो देवी मन्त्र

शं नो देवीर् अभिष्टय आपो भवन्तु पीतये ।
शं योर् अभिस्रवन्तु नः । ।। ऋ. 10-9-4 ।।

śaṃ nō dēvīr abhiṣṭaya āpō bhavantu pītayē
śaṃ yōr abhisravantu naḥ

May the divine waters be propitious to us. May the streams of good drinking-water be flowing to us for our preservation and health.

Health

आपः पृणीत भेषजं वरूथं तन्वे मम ।
ज्योक् च सूर्यं दृशे । ।। ऋ. 10-9-7 ।।

āpaḥ pṛṇīta bhēṣajaṃ varūthaṃ tanvē mama
jyōk ca sūryaṃ dṛśē

May waters be available for our crops. May waters be available for growing medicinal herbs which will keep us away from disease and afford us long life.

To the Spirit of the Dead

सं गच्छस्व पितृभिः सं यमेनेष्टापूर्तेन परमे व्योमन् ।
हित्वायावद्यं पुनर् अस्तमेहि सं गच्छस्व तन्वा सुवर्चाः ।।
।। ऋ. 10-14-8 ।।

saṃ gacchasva pitṛbhiḥ saṃ yamēnēṣṭāpūrtēna paramē vyōman
hitvāyāvadyaṃ punar astamēhi saṃ gacchasva tanvā suvarcāḥ

O Spirit of the dead! Go to the highest heaven and meet with Yama and your ancestors. Carry with you only the good karmas leaving behind the bad. Seek a body and a new home, and a life of glory.

Commentary

It is not clear whether this mantra conveys the seed of the theory of reincarnation. It appears to do so.

To the Widow

उदीर्ष्व नार्यभि जीवलोकं गतासुम् एतम् उप शेष एहि ।
हस्तग्राभस्य दिधिषोस् तवेदं पत्युर् जनित्वम् अभि सं बभूथ ।।
।। ऋ. 10-18-8 ।।

udīrṣva nāryabhi jīvalōkaṃ gatāsum ētam upa śēṣa ēhi
hastagrābhasya didhiṣōs tavēdaṃ patyur janitvam abhi saṃ babhūtha

Rise up O woman, to the world of the living. Your husband, is dead. Take the hand of a new man and start your life again.

Women

कियती योषा मर्यतो वधूयोः परिप्रीता पन्यसा वार्येण।
भद्रा वधूर् भवति यत् सुपेशाः स्वयं सा मित्रं वनुते जने चित्।।
।। ऋ. 10-27-12 ।।

kiyatī yōṣā maryatō vadhūyōḥ pariprītā panyasā vāryēṇa
bhadrā vadhūr bhavati yat supēśāḥ svayaṃ sā mitraṃ vanutē janē cit

Women feel good hearing the flattering admiration from men. Those who are gracious and beautiful get to choose the man of their choice.

Some women are trapped, into accepting a man by his sweet talk, but those who are smart, are careful in selecting their husband.

Commentary

This mantra clearly shows that in the Vedic times a girl had the freedom to decide who would be her husband.

Virtue

परि चिन् मर्तो द्रविणं ममन्याद् ऋतस्य पथा नमसा विवासेत्।
उत स्वेन क्रतुना सं वदेत श्रेयांसं दक्षं मनसा जगृभ्यात् ।।
।। ऋ. 10-31-2 ।।

pari cin martō draviṇaṃ mamanyād
ṛtasya pathā namasā vivāsēt
uta svēna kratunā saṃ vadēta
śrēyāṃsaṃ dakṣaṃ manasā jagṛbhyāt

May we achieve our desire for prosperity by moral means. May we seek advice from our conscience with a prayerful heart.

Obtaining Instructions

अक्षेत्रवित् क्षेत्रविदं ह्यप्राट् स प्रैति क्षेत्रविदानुशिष्टः ।
एतद् वै भद्रम् अनुशासनस् योत स्रुतिं विन्दत्यञ्जसीनाम् ।।
।। ऋ. 10-32-7 ।।

akṣētravit kṣētravidaṃ hyaprāṭ sa praiti kṣētravidānuśiṣṭaḥ
ētad vai bhadram anuśāsanas yōta srutiṃ vindatyañjasīnām

One who does not know the way should enquire of one who knows. Directed by the instructor he achieves his destination. Indeed, the benefit of obtaining instruction is that one may reach there by the straight path.

Gambling Addiction

न मा मिमेथ न जिहीळ एषा शिवा सखिभ्य उत मह्यम् आसीत् ।
अक्षस्याहम् एकपरस्य हेतोर् अनुव्रताम् अप जायाम् अरोधम् ।।
।। ऋ. 10-34-2 ।।

द्वेष्टि श्वश्रूरप जाया रुणद्धि न नाथितो विन्दते मर्डितारम् ।
अश्वस्येव जरतो वस्न्यस्य नाहं विन्दामि कितवस्य भोगम् ।।
।। ऋ. 10-34-3 ।।

na mā mimētha na jihiḷa ēṣā śivā sakhibhya uta mahyam āsīt
akṣasyāham ēkaparasya hētōr anuvratām apa jāyām arōdham

dvēṣṭi śvaśrūrapa jāyā ruṇaddhi na nāthitō vindatē marḍitāram
aśvasyēva jaratō vasnyasya nāhaṃ vindāmi kitavasya bhōgam

My wife is good natured. She never quarrelled with me. She was loving to me and kind to my friends. I have driven her away from me because of my addiction to gambling.

My wife has rejected me; and my mother-in-law dislikes me. No one is offering to help me – a compulsive gambler, who has lost everything. I am as unwanted as an old horse.

Gambling Addiction - continued

अक्षैर् मा दीव्यः कृषिम् इत् कृषस्व वित्ते रमस्व बहु मन्यमानः ।
तत्र गावः कितव तत्र जाया तन्मे वि चष्टे सवितायम् अर्यः ।।
।। ऋ. 10-34-13 ।।

akṣair mā dīvyaḥ kṛṣim it kṛṣasva vittē ramasva bahu manyamānaḥ
tatra gāvaḥ kitava tatra jāyā tanmē vi caṣṭē savitāyam aryaḥ

Do not play with dice. Till your land and rejoice in your income and property so obtained, feeling great about it. Consider yourself fortunate for possessing your cattle and having your wife with you. This is the message that Lord Savitar has revealed to me.

Prayer Seeking Protection

सविता पश्चातात् सविता पुरस्तात् सवितोत्तरात्तात् सविताधरात्तात् ।
सविता नः सुवतु सर्वतातिं सविता नो रासतां दीर्घम् आयुः ।।
।। ऋ. 10-36-14 ।।

savitā paścātāt savitā purastāt savitōttarāttāt savitādharāttāt
savitā naḥ suvatu sarvatātiṃ savitā nō rāsatāṃ dīrgham āyuḥ

Lord!
Protect us from the west;
Protect us from the east;
Protect us from the north;
Protect us from the south.
Grant us prosperity; and,
grant us long life.

Virtue

सा मा सत्योक्तिः परि पातु विश्वतो
द्यावा च यत्र ततनन्नहानि च ।
विश्वम् अन्यन् निविशते यदेजति
विश्वाहापो विश्वाहोदेति सूरयः ॥
॥ ऋ. 10-37-2 ॥

sā mā satyōktiḥ pari pātu viśvatō
dyāvā ca yatra tatanannahāni ca
viśvam anyan niviśatē yadējati
viśvāhāpō viśvāhōdēti sūrayaḥ

The Heaven and the Earth will endure.
The days will continue to be followed by nights.
The waters in the rivers will keep flowing.
The sun will keep rising.
And yet, every living being will come to rest.
While I live, may words of truth guard me and protect me on all sides.

Prayer Seeking Welfare

विश्वाहा त्वा सुमनसः सुचक्षसः प्रजावन्तो अनमीवा अनागसः ।
उद्यन्तं त्वा मित्रमहो दिवेदिवे ज्योग्जीवाः प्रति पश्येम सूर्य ।।
।। ऋ. 10-37-7 ।।

viśvāhā tvā sumanasaḥ sucakṣasaḥ
prajāvantō anamīvā anāgasaḥ
udyantaṃ tvā mitramahō divēdivē
jyōgjīvāḥ prati paśyēma sūrya

O Lord! Our Friend!

May we, always happy, sound of sight, blessed with family, free of sickness, devoid of sin, worship Thee everyday.

May we continue to witness the rising sun by being granted long life.

Work Ethic

गोभिष्टरेमामतिं दुरेवां यवेन क्षुधं पुरुहूत विश्वाम् ।
वयं राजभिः प्रथमा धनान्यस्माकेन वृजनेना जयेम ।।
।। ऋ. 10-43-10 ।।

gōbhiṣṭarēmāmatiṃ durēvāṃ yavēna kṣudhaṃ puruhūta viśvām
vayaṃ rājabhiḥ prathamā dhanānyasmākēna vṛjanēnā jayēma

God!
May we conquer poverty by removing ignorance.
May we conquer hunger by being productive.
May we conquer battles by being valiant.

Prayer Seeking Forgiveness

य ईशिरे भुवनस्य प्रचेतसो विश्वस्य स्थातुर् जगतश्च मन्तवः ।
ते नः कृताद् अकृताद् एनसस् पर्यद्या देवासः पिपृता स्वस्तये ।।
।। ऋ. 10-63-8 ।।

ya īśirē bhuvanasya pracētasō viśvasya sthātur jagataśca mantavaḥ
tē naḥ kṛtād akṛtād ēnasas paryadyā dēvāsaḥ pipṛtā svastayē

May the omniscient Lord who rules as Dēvas over the animate and the inanimate, deliver us today from our sins of the past and of future, for our own good.

Power of Speech

बृहस्पते प्रथमं वाचो अग्रं
यत् प्रैरत नामधेयं दधानाः ।
यद् एषां श्रेष्ठं यद् अरिप्रम् आसीत्
प्रेणा तद् एषां निहितं गुहाविः ।।
।। ऋ. 10-71-1 ।।

bṛhaspatē prathamaṃ vācō agraṃ
yat prairata nāmadhēyaṃ dadhānāḥ
yad ēṣāṃ śrēṣṭhaṃ yad aripram āsīt
prēṇā tad ēṣāṃ nihitaṃ guhāviḥ

With the power of speech that you granted us, we gave names to things, O Lord!

You lovingly gave us the power to speak what is noble, and what without speech would be hidden in secrecy.

Discretion in Speech

सक्तुम् इव तितउना पुनन्तो यत्र धीरा मनसा वाचम् अक्रत ।
अत्रा सखायः सख्यानि जानते भद्रैषां लक्ष्मीर् निहिताधि वाचि ॥
॥ ऋ. 10-71-2 ॥

saktum iva titaunā punantō yatra dhīrā manasā vācam akrata
atrā sakhāyaḥ sakhyāni jānatē bhadraiṣāṃ lakṣmīr nihitādhi vāci

Farmers use a sieve to separate out grain from chaff. Wise men use discretion as the sieve to speak only what should be spoken. The inner grace of a person shows up through the words spoken by him. It is through speech that great friendships are founded.

Discretion in Speech

उत त्वं सख्ये स्थिरपीतम् आहुर् नैनं हिन्वन्त्यपि वाजिनेषु ।
अधेन्वा चरति माययैष वाचं शुश्रुवाँ अफलाम् अपुष्पाम् ॥
॥ ऋ. 10-71-5 ॥

uta tvaṃ sakhyē sthirapītam āhur nainaṃ hinvantyapi vājinēṣu
adhēnvā carati māyayaiṣa vācaṃ śuśruvām̐ aphalām apuṣpām

In the company of learned people, the one who uses his faculty of speech meaningfully, courteously, and discretely, is called an able person. On the contrary, the person who opens his mouth fruitlessly, creating a lot of heat but no light, is like a cow that does not yield any milk, or like a tree that does not bear flowers and fruit.

Recognising a Friend

यस् तित्याज सचिविदं सखायं न तस्य वाच्यपि भागो अस्ति ।
यदीं श्रृणोत्यलकं शृणोति न हि प्रवेद सुकृतस्य पन्थाम् ।।
।। ऋ. 10-71-6 ।।

yas tityāja sacividaṃ sakhāyaṃ na tasya vācyapi bhāgō asti
yadīṃ śṛṛṇōtyalakaṃ śṛṇōti na hi pravēda sukṛtasya panthām

The person who rejects a wise friend (advisor) is not only the one who lacks grace in speech, but who fails to hear what is good for him. He is the one who does not find the path chosen by successful people.

Intellect

अक्षण्वन्तः कर्णवन्तः सखायो मनोजवेष्वसमा बभूवुः ।
आदघ्नास उपकक्षास उ त्वे ह्रदा इव स्नात्वा उ त्वे ददृश्रे ।।
।। ऋ. 10-71-7 ।।

akṣaṇvantaḥ karṇavantaḥ sakhāyō manōjavēṣvasamā babhūvuḥ
ādaghnāsa upakakṣāsa u tvē hradā iva snātvā u tvē dadṛśrē

Various pools of water may look alike, but some may be knee-deep and others may be much deeper. In the same way most people may appear to be equally endowed with eyes and ears, and yet their natural abilities to absorb wisdom imparted by an instructor may be very different.

Creation

किं स्विदासीद् अधिष्ठानम् आरम्भणं कतमत् स्वित् कथासीत् ।
यतो भूमिं जनयन् विश्वकर्मा वि द्यामौर्णोन्महिना विश्वचक्षाः ।।
।। ऋ. 10-81-2 ।।

kiṃ svidāsīd adhiṣṭhānam ārambhaṇaṃ katamat svit kathāsīt
yatō bhūmiṃ janayan viśvakarmā vi dyāmaurṇōnmahinā viśvacakṣāḥ

The all-knowing Lord created the earth and the sky using his divine powers. How he began and accomplished it, is a question which has not been answered yet.

Omnipresent God

विश्वतश् चक्षुर् उत विश्वतोमुखो विश्वतोबाहुर् उत विश्वतस् पात् ।
सं बाहुभ्यां धमति सं पतत्रैर् द्यावा भूमी जनयन् देव एकः ।।
।। ऋ. 10-81-3 ।।

viśvataś cakṣur uta viśvatōmukhō
viśvatōbāhur uta viśvatas pāt
saṃ bāhubhyāṃ dhamati saṃ patatrair
dyāvā bhūmī janayan dēva ēkaḥ

The Supreme Lord has his eyes in every direction. His hands stretch out to reach every place. With His feet He instantaneously reaches everywhere. He is the one who has created this whole universe. He is the One and only, who rewards and punishes.

Commentary

Śvētāśvatara Upaniṣad verse 3-3 is an identical copy of this verse.

One God

यो नः पिता जनिता यो विधाता धामानि वेद भुवनानि विश्वा ।
यो देवानां नामधा एक एव तं संप्रश्नं भुवना यन्त्यन्या ॥
॥ ऋ. 10-82-3 ॥

yō naḥ pitā janitā yō vidhātā dhāmāni vēda bhuvanāni viśvā
yō dēvānāṃ nāmadhā ēka ēva taṃ sampraśnaṃ bhuvanā yantyanyā

Many people ask who God is. He is our parent and ruler. He is our preserver. He knows everything and everyone. All the deities are Him, the One and only. Yet, human beings keep asking who he is.

Divinity in Man

न तं विदाथ य इमा जजानान्यद् युष्माकम् अन्तरं बभूव ।
नीहारेण प्रावृता जल्प्या चासुतृप उक्थशासश् चरन्ति ।।
।। ऋ. 10-82-7 ।।

na taṃ vidātha ya imā jajānānyad yuṣmākam antaraṃ babhūva
nihārēṇa prāvṛtā jalpyā cāsutṛpa ukthaśāsaś caranti

O men! You do not know the Supreme Lord who has created all the stars and the planets, and all the living beings. You, yourself, have within you the divine element.

Ignorant persons remain satisfied with acquiring their physical needs and with chanting the mantras without understanding what they represent. These men are unable to reach the divine within.

Commentary

This Ṛgvedic hymn is extremely important, in that it, perhaps, was the inspiration for the philosophy of the Upaniṣads. In the Upaniṣads, the divine element mentioned in this hymn was expounded as the individual soul and as part of the Supreme Soul. Also this mantra stresses the need for acquiring wisdom which is the central theme of the Upaniṣads. It is remarkable to observe here that countless Hindūs and men of other faiths read or chant parts of their scriptures without understanding their meaning. Many Hindūs even chant verses and so-called mantras which are not true scriptures and have undesirable meanings and consequences, simply because they have not cared to know the meaning of what they are chanting.

Wedding guests

अनृक्षरा ऋजवः सन्तु पन्था येभिः सखायो यन्ति नो वरेयम् ।
समर्यमा सं भगो नो निनीयात् सं जास्पत्यं सुयमम् अस्तु देवाः ।।
।। ऋ. 10-85-23 ।।

anṛkṣarā ṛjavaḥ santu panthā
yēbhiḥ sakhāyō yanti nō varēyam
samaryamā saṃ bhagō nō nirīyāt saṃ
jāspatyaṃ suyamam astu dēvāḥ

Smooth and troublefree be the paths on which our well-wishers travel to attend the wedding ceremony. May the wedding ceremony be smoothly accomplished. May the Dēvas make this union strong.

Blessing to the Bride

पूषा त्वेतो नयतु हस्तगृह्याश्विना त्वा प्र वहतां रथेन ।
गृहान् गच्छ गृहपत्नी यथासो वशिनी त्वं विदथमा वदासि ।।
।। ऋ. 10-85-26 ।।

pūṣā tvētō nayatu hastagṛhyāśvinā tvā pra vahatāṃ rathēna
gṛhān gaccha gṛhapatnī yathāsō vaśinī tvaṃ vidathamā vadāsi

May Dēva Pūṣan himself lead you by hand from here. May the Aśvins carry you in their own chariot, O bride! Go to your new home to become the ruler of the house, with authority in your voice.

Blessing to the Bride

इह प्रियं प्रजया ते समृध्यताम् अस्मिन् गृहे गार्हपत्याय जागृहि ।
एना पत्या तन्वं सं सृजस्वाधा जिव्री विदथमा वदाथः ।।
।। ऋ. 10-85-27 ।।

iha priyaṃ prajayā tē samṛdhyatām asmin gṛhē gārhapatyāya jāgṛhi
ēnā patyā tanvaṃ saṃ sṛjasvādhā jivrī vidathamā vadāthaḥ

O Bride! May happiness attend you in your new home. May love increase as you bear children. Unite your person with that of your husband and continue to rule over the household all your life.

सुमङ्गलीर् इयं वधूर् इमां समेत पश्यत ।
सौभाग्यम् अस्यै दत्त्वायाथास्तं वि परेतन ।।
।। ऋ. 10-85-33 ।।

sumaṅgalīr iyaṃ vadhūr imāṃ samēta paśyata
saubhāgyam asyai dattvāyāthāstaṃ vi parētana

Let this bride be attended with good fortune. Before you (the guests) depart for your home, come one and all to meet her and wish her happiness.

Man to Woman

गृभ्णामि ते सौभगत्वाय हस्तं मया पत्या जरदष्टिर्यथासः ।
भगो अर्यमा सविता पुरन्धिर् मह्यं त्वादुर् गार्हपत्याय देवाः ।।
।। ऋ. 10-85-36 ।।

gṛbhṇāmi tē saubhagatvāya hastaṃ
mayā patyā jaradaṣṭiryathāsaḥ
bhagō aryamā savitā purandhir mahyaṃ
tvādur gārhapatyāya dēvāḥ

I take thy hand in mine for good fortune; that thou mayest live to old age with me, thy husband. Dēvas Bhaga, Aryamā, and the bounteous Savitā have given thee to me, for you to become the ruler of my house.

Commentary

The word purandhi has been misunderstood to be a Dēva by many translators.

Blessing to the Bride

पुनः पत्नीम् अग्निर् अदाद् आयुषा सह वर्चसा ।
दीर्घायुर् अस्या यः पतिर् जीवाति शरदः शतम् ।।
।। ऋ. 10-85-39 ।।

punaḥ patnīm agnir adād āyuṣā saha varcasā
dīrghāyur asyā yaḥ patir jīvāti śaradaḥ śatam

O Bride! In the presence of the sacred fire have you been given to your husband. May you live long and may your life be filled with glory. May your husband see a hundred summers.

Blessing the Newlyweds

इहैव स्तं मा वि यौष्टं विश्वम् आयुर् व्यश्नुतम् ।
क्रीळन्तौ पुत्रैर् नप्तृभिर् मोदमानौ स्वे गृहे ।।
।। ऋ. 10-85-42 ।।

ihaiva staṃ mā vi yauṣṭaṃ viśvam āyur vyaśnutam
krīḷantau putrair naptṛbhir mōdamānau svē gṛhē

O newly married couple!

May you make a stable family, never to separate.

Enjoy the full span of life, happy, sporting with children and grandchildren.

Blessing the Bride

सम्राज्ञी श्वशुरे भव सम्राज्ञी श्वश्र्वां भव ।
ननान्दरि सम्राज्ञी भव सम्राज्ञी अधि देवृषु ॥
॥ ऋ. 10-85-46 ॥

samrājñī śvaśurē bhava samrājñī śvaśravāṃ bhava
nanāndari samrājñī bhava samrājñī adhi dēvṛṣu

O Bride!
May your father-in-law treat you as a queen.
May your mother-in-law treat you as a queen.
May the sisters and brothers of your husband treat you as a queen.

Prayer by Bride and Groom

समञ्जन्तु विश्वे देवाः समापो हृदयानि नौ ।
सं मातरिश्वा सं धाता समु देष्ट्री दधातु नौ ।।
।। ऋ. 10-85-47 ।।

samañjantu viśvē dēvāḥ samāpō hṛdayāni nau
saṃ mātariśvā saṃ dhātā samu dēṣṭrī dadhātu nau

May all the angels unite our hearts. May the flowing waters unite our hearts. May Mātariśvan and Sarasvatī unite our hearts.

Puruṣa-sūkta (10-90)

This sūkta was considered very seriously for inclusion. After great deliberation it was decided not to include it.

Glory to Śrī Rāma

प्र तद्दुःशीमे पृथवाने वेने प्र रामे वोचमसुरे मघवत्सु ।
ये युक्त्वाय पञ्च शतास्मयु पथा विश्राव्येषाम् ।।
।। ऋ. 10-93-14 ।।

pra tadduḥśīmē pṛthavānē vēnē pra rāmē vōcamasurē maghavatsu
yē yuktvāya pañca śatāsmayu pathā viśrāvyēṣām

I say my prayer in the presence of kings Duḥśīma, Pṛthu, Vēna, and the mighty king Rāma to whose chariot are yoked five hundred horses and whose renown is spread in all directions.

Commentary

King Rāma mentioned in this Ṛgvēda mantra is none other than Śrī Rāma, the son of King Daśaratha.

Helping One Another

अन्या वो अन्याम् अवतु, अन्यान्यस्या उपावत ।
ताः सर्वाः संविदाना इदं मे प्रावता वचः ।।
।। ऋ. 10-97-14 ।।

anyā vō anyām avatu, anyānyasyā upāvata
tāḥ sarvāḥ saṃvidānā idaṃ mē prāvatā vacaḥ

Let us be helpful to others.
Let us lend as much assistance to others as possible.
Let us be cordial to others.

Charity

दैवी पूर्तिर् दक्षिणा देवयज्या न कवारिभ्यो नहि ते पृणन्ति ।
अथा नरः प्रयत दक्षिणा सोऽवद्यभिया बहवः पृणन्ति ।।
।। ऋ. 10-107-3 ।।

daivī pūrtir dakṣiṇā dēvayajyā na kavāribhyō nahi tē pṛṇanti
athā naraḥ prayata dakṣiṇā sō'vadyabhiyā bahavaḥ pṛṇanti

Charity to the needy is a good way of worshipping the Lord. It is a blessing and a privilege which is not available to non-believers and those who indulge in sinful actions. Prayers and worship by sinners do not please God. Only those who stay away from sins and from denigrating others and make a pious gift to God are the ones who are able to please God.

Commentary

This is one of most remarkable mantras of Ṛgvēda Saṃhitā. Many people mistakenly believe that they can indulge in sinful actions day after day and by occasionally worshipping God they will be forgiven. This mantra says that their worship will not please God. Worship must be accompanied by fulfilment of duty and giving of gifts to God. What can you give to God who has given everything to you? Serving the sick, the helpless, and the less fortunate with your time and money is the way to give gifts to God. One must see God in the faces of the suffering people.

One God

सुपर्णं विप्राः कवयो वचोभिर् एकं सन्तं बहुधा कल्पयन्ति ।।
।। ऋ. 10-114-5 ।।

suparṇaṃ viprāḥ kavayō vacōbhir ēkaṃ santaṃ bahudhā kalpayanti

The wise seers in their adoration make into many forms the One Supreme.

Charity

न वा उ देवाः क्षुधम् इद् वधं
दुदुर् उत् आशितम् उप गच्छन्ति मृत्यवः ।
उतो रयिः पृणतो नोप दस्यत्युतापृणन्
मर्डितारं न विन्दते ।।
।। ऋ. 10-117-1 ।।

na vā u dēvāḥ kṣudham id vadhaṃ
dadur ut āśitam upa gacchanti mṛtyavaḥ
utō rayiḥ pṛṇatō nōpa dasyatyutāpṛṇan
marḍitāraṃ na vindatē

(Remember, you rich persons!)

The poor and the hungry are not the only ones who die. The rich and well-fed die too. The wealth of the rich man who generously gives, does not run out. On the other hand the world has no sympathy for the rich person who does not give.

Charity

मोघम् अन्नं विन्दते अप्रचेताः सत्यं ब्रवीमि वध इत् स तस्य ।
नार्यमणं पुष्यति नो सखायं केवलाघो भवति केवलादी ।।
।। ऋ. 10-117-6 ।।

mōgham annaṃ vindatē apracētāḥ satyaṃ bravīmi vadha it sa tasya
nāryamaṇaṃ puṣyati nō sakhāyaṃ kēvalāghō bhavati kēvalādī

The inhospitable person acquires wealth in vain. I tell you sincerely that he is working on his own downfall. He is in favor with neither God nor men. The rich person who does not share is a sinner.

Prayer Singing Glory

हिरण्यगर्भः समवर्तताग्रे भूतस्य जातः पतिरेक आसीत् ।
स दाधार पृथिवीं द्याम् उतेमां कस्मै देवाय हविषा विधेम ।।
।। ऋ. 10-121-1 ।।

hiraṇyagarbhaḥ samavartatāgrē bhūtasya jātaḥ patirēka āsīt
sa dādhāra pṛthivīṃ dyām utēmāṃ kasmai dēvāya haviṣā vidhēma

What God shall we worship with our oblations?

The One who existed in the beginning and who is the prime cause of the elements; the One who upholds the Earth and the Sky; the One who is the lord of all living beings.

Prayer Singing Glory

य आत्मदा बलदा यस्य विश्व उपासते प्रशिषं यस्य देवाः ।
यस्य छायामृतं यस्य मृत्युः कस्मै देवाय हविषा विधेम ।।
।। ऋ. 10-121-2 ।।

ya ātmadā baladā yasya viśva upāsatē praśiṣaṃ yasya dēvāḥ
yasya chāyāmṛtaṃ yasya mṛtyuḥ kasmai dēvāya haviṣā vidhēma

What God shall we worship with our oblations?
The One who is the bestower of life and vigor;
the One whose commandments the cosmic forces carry out;
the One who bestows immortality or death.

यः प्राणतो निमिषतो महित्वैक इद्राजा जगतो बभूव ।
य ईशे अस्य द्विपदश् चतुष्पदः कस्मै देवाय हविषा विधेम ।।
।। ऋ. 10-121-3 ।।

yaḥ prāṇatō nimiṣatō mahitvaika idrājā jagatō babhūva
ya īśē asya dvipadaś catuṣpadaḥ kasmai dēvāya haviṣā vidhēma

What God shall we worship with our oblations?

The One who, by his power and greatness, rules eternally over men and animals, all of whom assume life for a fleeting moment.

Prayer Singing Glory

येन द्यौर् उग्रा पृथिवी च दृळहा येन स्वः स्तभितं येन नाकः ।
यो अन्तरिक्षे रजसो विमानः कस्मै देवाय हविषा विधेम ।।
।। ऋ. 10-121-5 ।।

yēna dyaur ugrā pṛthivī ca dṛḷahā yēna svaḥ stabhitaṃ yēna nākaḥ
yō antarikṣē rajasō vimānaḥ kasmai dēvāya haviṣā vidhēma

What God shall we worship with our oblations?

The One who made the solid earth and the vast sky;

The One who runs the solar system and makes water go up to become rain clouds.

Prayer Seeking Welfare

प्रजापते न त्वदेतान्यन्यो विश्वा जातानि परि ता बभूव ।
यत् कामास् ते जुहुमस् तन् नो अस्तु वयं स्याम पतयो रयीणाम् ।।
।। ऋ. 10-121-10 ।।

prajāpatē na tvadētānyanyō viśvā jātāni pari tā babhūva
yat kāmās tē juhumas tan nō astu vayaṃ syāma patayō rayīṇām

O lord of all! None except you pervades everything and every being. May our wishes, for which we have come to pray you, be granted. May we become happy and prosperous.

Prayer Seeking Virtue

मह्यं यजन्तु मम यानि हव्याकूतिः सत्या मनसो मे अस्तु ।
एनो मा नि गां कतमच्चनाहं विश्वेदेवासो अधि वोचता नः ।।
।। ऋ. 10-128-4 ।।

mahyaṃ yajantu mama yāni havyākūtiḥ satyā manasō mē astu
ēnō mā ni gāṃ katamaccanāhaṃ viśvēdēvāsō adhi vōcatā naḥ

May my priest offer my oblations to God. May the purpose of my mind be sincere. May I not fall into any kind of sin. May I be blessed by Dēvas.

Creation

नासदीय सूक्त

नासद् आसीन् नोसद् आसीत् तदानीं
नासीद् रजो नो व्योमा परो यत् ।
किम् आवरीवः कुह कस्य
शर्मन्नम्भः किम् आसीद् गहनं गभीरम् ॥
॥ ऋ. 10-129-1 ॥

nāsad āsīn nōsad āsīt tadānīṃ
nāsīd rajō nō vyōmā parō yat
kim āvarīvaḥ kuha kasya
śarmannambhaḥ kim āsīd gahanaṃ gabhīram

Nāsadīya Hymn

In the beginning there was neither existence nor non-existence. There was neither air nor space. There was no water, deep and fathomless. There was nothing to envelope or protect.

न मृत्युर् आसीद् अमृतं न तर्हि न रात्र्या अह्न आसीत् प्रकेतः ।
आनीद् अवातं स्वधया तद् एकं तस्माद् हान्यन् नपरः किं चनास ।।
।। ऋ. 10-129-2 ।।

na mṛtyur āsīd amṛtaṃ na tarhi na
rātryā ahna āsīt prakētaḥ
ānīd avātaṃ svadhayā tad ēkaṃ tasmād
hānyan naparaḥ kiṃ canāsa

There was neither death nor immortality. There was neither night nor day. Only God breathed windless by his own power. Apart from God there was nothing whatsoever.

तम आसीत् तमसा गूळहमग्रेऽप्रकेतं सलिलं सर्वमा इदम् ।
तुच्छ्येनाभ्वपिहितं यद् आसीत् तपसस् तन् महिनाजायतैकम् ।।
।। ऋ. 10-129-3 ।।

tama āsīt tamasā gūḷahamagrē'prakētaṃ
salilaṃ sarvamā idam
tucchyēnābhvapihitaṃ yad āsīt
tapasas tan mahinājāyataikam

Darkness prevailed everywhere before the creation of the universe. Yet there subsisted one glorious Being, all intelligence, who created the universe by contemplation of what he wanted to do.

को अद्धा वेद क इह प्र वोचत् कुत आजाता कुत इयं विसृष्टिः ।
अर्वाग्देवा अस्य विसर्जनेनाथा को वेद यत आबभूव ।।
।। ऋ. 10-129-6 ।।

kō addhā vēda ka iha pra vōcat kuta ājātā kuta iyaṃ visṛṣṭiḥ
arvāgdēvā asya visarjanēnāthā kō vēda yata ābabhūva

We men do not really know. Who can therefore tell, how this universe was created and when? Even the angels may have come into existence after the universe was created. No one can tell.

इयं विसृष्टिर् यत आबभूव यदि वा दधे यदि वा न ।
यो अस्याध्यक्षः परमे व्योमन्त्सो अङ्ग वेद यदि वा न वेद ।।
(अथ को वेद ?) ।। ऋ. 10-129-7 ।।

iyaṃ visṛṣṭir yata ābabhūva yadi vā dadhē yadi vā na
yō asyādhyakṣaḥ paramē vyōmantsō aṅga vēda yadi vā na vēda
(atha kō vēda ?)

Some people ask, "Did the elemental matter, from which this universe was built, always exist or was it also created by God?"

The One who built and who controls the universe alone knows. If He does not know then who knows?

Prayer Seeking Virtue

यद् आशसा निःशसाभिशसोपारिम जाग्रतो यत् स्वपन्तः ।
अग्निर् विश्वान्यप दुष्कृतान्यजुष्टान्यारे अस्मद् दधातु ।।
।। ऋ. 10-164-3 ।।

yad āśasā niḥśasābhiśasōpārima jāgratō yat svapantaḥ
agnir viśvānyapa duṣkṛtānyajuṣṭānyārē asmad dadhātu

Whatever sins we have committed in speaking to others, and in speaking of others, on purpose or inadvertently, in dream or when wide awake, O Lord! please remove far away from us such unworthy acts in future.

Truth and Righteousness

ऋतं च सत्यं चाभीद्धात् तपसोऽध्यजायत ।
ततो रात्र्यजायत ततः समुद्रो अर्णवः ।।
।। ऋ. 10-190-1 ।।

ṛtaṃ ca satyaṃ cābhīddhāt tapasō'dhyajāyata
tatō rātryajāyata tataḥ samudrō arṇavaḥ

Arduous prayers have given birth to truth and righteousness. It is as if the blistering heat has given birth to the cool night and foaming waters of the sea.

Commentary

The above is a generous translation because the strict translation does not seem to connect.

Creation

सूर्या चन्द्रमसौ धाता यथापूर्वं अकल्पयत् ।
दिवं च पृथिवीं चान्तरिक्षम् अथो स्वः ।। ऋ. 10-190-3 ।।

sūryā candramasau dhātā yathāpūrvaṃ akalpayat
divaṃ ca pṛthivīṃ cāntarikṣam athō svaḥ

Systematically, Lord, the creator, brought forth the sun, and the moon, the heaven, and the earth, the atmosphere, and the days and nights.

Unity and Togetherness

सं गच्छध्वं सं वदध्वं सं वो मनांसि जानताम् ।
देवा भागं यथा पूर्वे संजानाना उपासते ।। ऋ. 10-191-2 ।।

saṃ gacchadhvaṃ saṃ vadadhvaṃ saṃ vō manāṃsi jānatām
dēvā bhāgaṃ yathā pūrvē saṃjānānā upāsatē

Congregate. Speak with one another. Bring your minds into accord. Pray together as the sages in the past always did.

Unity and Togetherness.

समानोमन्त्रः समितिः समानी समानं मनः सह चित्तम् एषाम् ।
समानं मन्त्रम् अभिमन्त्रये वः समानेन वो हविषा जुहोमि ।।
।। ऋ. 10-191-3 ।।

samānōmantraḥ samitiḥ samānī samānaṃ manaḥ saha cittam ēṣām
samānaṃ mantram abhimantrayē vaḥ samānēna vō haviṣā juhōmi

May our assembly be common;
may our minds be common;
may our prayers be common, and
may our purpose be common.
With these wishes we offer Thee our oblations.

समानी व आकूतिः समाना हृदयानि वः ।
समानम् अस्तु वो मनो यथा वः सुसहासति ।।
।। ऋ. 10-191-4 ।।

samānī va ākūtiḥ samānā hṛdayāni vaḥ
samānam astu vō manō yathā vaḥ susahāsati

United be our resolves;
united be our hearts;
united be our spirits.
May we live together (in a nation) in unity and brotherhood.

II

यजुर्वेद
(वाजसनेयी-संहिता)
The Yajurvēda
(Vājasanēyī-saṃhitā)

Adhyāya 1

Prayer Seeking Virtue

अग्ने व्रतपते व्रतं चरिष्यामि तच्छकेयं तन्मे राध्यताम् ।
इदम् अहम् अनृतात् सत्यम् उपैमि ।। ।। य. 1-5 ।।

agnē vratapatē vrataṃ cariṣyāmi tacchakēyaṃ tanmē rādhyatām
idam aham anṛtāt satyam upaimi

O lord and master of your will!

Give me the strength of determination,

That I may succeed

In moving away from the darkness of untruth

To the light of truth.

---

* The material here is drawn from the Śukla Yajurvēda, also known as Vājasanēyī Saṃhitā. In Vājasanēyī Saṃhitā there are two rescensions which differ in minor details. The material here is based on the most accepted rescension known as Mādhyandina. Kṛṣṇa Yajurvēda is the older of the two major Yajurvēda versions. It contains additional matter to what is contained in Śukla Yajurvēda. Also throughout the text the two differ in minor details. Most of Yajurvēda is in prose in contrast to Ṛgvēda which is all in verse.

Adhyāya 2

Prayer Seeking Good Life

सं वर्‌चसा पयसा सं तनूभिर् अगन्‌महि मनसा सꣳ शिवेन ।
त्वष्टा सुदत्रो विदधातु रायोऽनुमार्ष्टु तन्वो यद्विलिष्टम् ॥
॥ य. 2-24 ॥

saṃ varcasā payasā saṃ tanūbhir aganmahi manasā saṃ śivēna
tvaṣṭā sudatrō vidadhātu rāyō'numārṣṭu tanvō yadviliṣṭam

O Lord!
Grant us prosperity.
Grant us the gift of undecaying body.
Grant us physical strength and purity of mind.
Grant us a life of glory.

Adhyāya 3

Prayer Seeking Welfare

तनूपा अग्नेऽसि तन्वं मे पाह्यायुर्दा अग्नेस्यायुर्मे देहि ।
वर्चो दा अग्नेऽसि वर्चो मे देहि ।
अग्ने यन् मे तन्वा ऊनं तन् म आपृण ।। य. 3-17 ।।

tanūpā agnē'si tanvaṃ mē pāhyāyurdā agnēsyāyurmē dēhi
varcō dā agnē'si varcō mē dēhi
agnē yan mē tanvā ūnaṃ tan ma āpṛṇa

Lord!
You are the protector; protect me.
You are the giver of life; give me long life.
You provide the intelligence; provide me with a sharp mind.
You know what I lack; grant that to me.

Prayer Seeking Good Life

सम् अहम् आयुषा सं वर्चसा सं प्रजया सꣳ रायस् पोषेण
ग्मिषीय । ॥ य. 3-19 ॥

sam aham āyuṣā saṃ varcasā saṃ prajayā saṃ rāyas pōṣēṇa gmiṣīya

O Lord!

I pray to you to grant me long life, intelligence, good offspring, and prosperity.

Home – Prayer by the Visitors

येषाम् अध्येति प्रवसन् येषु सौमनसो बहुः ।
गृहान् उपह्वयामहे ते नो जानन्तु जानतः ॥ य. 3-42 ॥

yēṣām adhyēti pravasan yēṣu saumanasō bahuḥ
gṛhān upahvayāmahē tē nō jānantu jānataḥ

O Lord! Let this home be one in which love abounds, such that a person visiting this home always remembers it.

Let us be welcome in this home.

Adhyāya 4

Prayer Seeking Virtue

परिमाग्ने दुश्चरिताद् बाधस्वा मा सुचरिते भज ।
उद् आयुषा स्वायुषोदस्थाम् अमृताँ २ अनु ।। य. 4-28 ।।

parimāgnē duścaritād bādhasvā mā sucaritē bhaja
ud āyuṣā svāyuṣōdasthām amṛtām̐ anu

Bar me O Lord, against evil conduct.
Make me a sharer in good conduct.
I have risen up with good life following the angels.

Adhyāya 5

Prayer to Viṣṇu

विष्णो रराटमसि विष्णोः श्नप्त्रे स्थो विष्णोः स्यूरसि विष्णोर्
ध्रुवोऽसि ।
वैष्णवमसि विष्णवे त्वा । ।। य. 5-21 ।।

viṣṇō rarāṭamasi viṣṇōḥ śnaptrē sthō viṣṇōḥ syūrasi viṣṇōr dhruvō'si
vaiṣṇavamasi viṣṇavē tvā

O Lord Viṣṇu! You are the crown upon the head of all the actions we perform. You are the spokesperson of the universe. You are the world and the space. You are the knot which ties the universe. The entire universe is strung together and upheld by you.

O my heart! I dedicate you this day to Viṣṇu, the lord of the universe.

Adhyāya 6

Blessing to a Younger Person

चक्षुस् त आ प्यायतां,
श्रोत्रं त आ प्यायतां,
वाक् त आ प्यायतां,
मनस् त आ प्यायतां,
प्राणस् त आ प्यायतां । || य. 6-15 ||*

cakṣus ta ā pyāyatāṃ,
śrōtraṃ ta ā pyāyatāṃ,
vāk ta ā pyāyatāṃ,
manas ta ā pyāyatāṃ,
prāṇas ta ā pyāyatāṃ

May you see all that needs to be seen,
May you listen to all that needs to be listened,
May you speak what needs to be spoken,
May your thinking be wholesome,
May you lead yourself to perfection.

* Partial and rearranged.

Prayer Seeking Contentment and Peace

मनो मे तर्पयत, वाचं मे तर्पयत, प्राणं मे तर्पयत,
चक्षुर् मे तर्पयत, श्रोत्रं मे तर्पयत,
आत्मानं मे तर्पयत, प्रजां मे तर्पयत,
पशून् मे तर्पयत, गणान् मे तर्पयत,
गणा मे मा वि तृषन् । ।। य. 6-31 ।।

manō mē tarpayata, vācaṃ mē tarpayata, prāṇaṃ mē tarpayata,
cakṣur mē tarpayata, śrōtraṃ mē tarpayata,
ātmānaṃ mē tarpayata, prajāṃ mē tarpayata,
paśūn mē tarpayata, gaṇān mē tarpayata,
gaṇā mē mā vi tṛṣan

O Lord! Let contentment come to
- my mind;
- my speech;
- my breath;
- my eyes;
- my ears;
- my soul;
- my progeny; and to
- the people around me.

Let the people around me never suffer a longing of any kind.

Adhyāya 8

Prayer Seeking Mental Power

देवा गातुविदो गातुं वित्त्वा गातुमित ।
मनसस्पत इमं देव यज्ञꣳ स्वाहा वाते धाः ।। य. 8-21 ।।

dēvā gātuvidō gātuṃ vittvā gātumita
manasaspata imaṃ dēva yajñaṃ svāhā vātē dhāḥ

O Dēvas! The rulers of minds!

I do not want a limited growth of my mental powers;

I seek your blessings in my wish for an unimpeded growth of my mental faculties.

Adhyāya 11

Noble Thoughts and Actions

देव सवितः प्र सुव यज्ञं, प्र सुव यज्ञपतिं भगाय ।
दिव्यो गन्धर्वः केतपूः केतं नः पुनातु वाचस्पतिर् वाचं नः
स्वदतु । ।। य. 11-7 ।।

dēva savitaḥ pra suva yajñaṃ, pra suva yajñapatiṃ bhagāya
divyō gandharvaḥ kētapūḥ kētaṃ naḥ punātu vācaspatir
vācaṃ naḥ svadatu

O Lord!

Fill in us the desire to offer worship to you.

Make us cherish only those desires which are noble.

Make us utter only those words which are pure, clean, and cordial.

Adhyāya 13

God's Generosity

भूरसि भूमिरस्यदितिरसि विश्वधाया विश्वस्य भुवनस्य धर्त्री ।
पृथिवीं यच्छ पृथिवीं दृꣳह पृथिवीं मा हिꣳसीः ।। य. 13-18 ।।

bhūrasi bhūmirasyaditirasi viśvadhāyā viśvasya bhuvanasya dhartrī
pṛthivīṃ yaccha pṛthivīṃ dṛṃha pṛthivīṃ mā hiṃsīḥ

Our Earth!
This our earth is immense.
It provides us abundance.
It is all sustaining — all nourishing;
It has room for entire mankind whom it so graciously supports.
We can see clearly that our earth is not hostile to us.

Adhyāya 14

God's Generosity

मूर्धाऽसि राड् ध्रुवाऽसि धरुणा धर्त्र्यसि धरणी ।
आयुषे त्वा वर्चसे त्वा कृष्यै त्वा क्षेमाय त्वा ।। य. 14-21 ।।

mūrdhā'si rāḍ dhruvā'si dharuṇā dhartryasi dharaṇī
āyuṣē tvā varcasē tvā kṛṣyai tvā kṣēmāya tvā

O Earth!
You are the stable support of all beings.
You preserve our lives.
You grant us vigor; and you provide us a place to abide, and to cultivate our crops.

Adhyāya 15

Service of Others

उद्बुध्यस्वाग्ने प्रति जागृहि त्वमिष्टापूर्ते सꣳ सृजेथामयं च ।
असि्मन्त्सधस्थे अध्युत्तरसि्मन् विश्वे देवा यजमानश्च सीदत ।।
।। य. 15-54 ।।

udbudhyasvāgnē prati jāgṛhi tvamiṣṭāpūrtē saṃ sṛjēthāmayaṃ ca
asmintsadhasthē adhyuttavarasmin viśvē dēvā yajamānaśca sīdata

O Agni!

The seated Yajamāna (host) is sharing the worship with us (while bearing the entire cost of the worship ceremony).

His family has set a superior example, among us, of personal piety and actions in the service of others.

We ask the Dēvas to wake all of us up to our sense of piety and service of others.

Adhyāya 16

Prayer Singing Glory

नमः शम्भवाय च
मयोभवाय च
नमः शंकराय च
मयस्कराय च
नमः शिवाय च
शिवतराय च । || य. 16-41 ||

namaḥ śambhavāya ca
mayōbhavāya ca
namaḥ śaṅkarāya ca
mayaskarāya ca
namaḥ śivāya ca
śivatarāya ca

Salutations to you O God!
- the granter of welfare;
- the source of happiness;
- the beneficent;
- the cause of joy;
- the auspicious;
- the source of greatest bliss.

Adhyāya 17

Devotion

यस्य कुर्मो गृहे हविस्तमग्ने वर्धया त्वम् ।
तस्मै देवा अधि ब्रुवन्नयं च ब्रह्मणस्पतिः ।। य. 17-52 ।।

yasya kurmō gr̥hē havistamagnē vardhayā tvam
tasmai dēvā adhi bruvannayaṃ ca brahmaṇaspatiḥ

God bestows prosperity on the person who worships. God blesses such a person. The worshipper is the one who can be called wise.

Adhyāya 18

Prayer Seeking Good Life

वाजश्च मे, प्रसवश्च मे, प्रयतिश्च मे, प्रसितिश्च मे,
धीतिश्च मे, क्रतुश्च मे, स्वरश्च मे, श्लोकश्च मे,
श्रवश्च मे, श्रुतिश्च मे, ज्योतिश्च मे,
स्वश्च मे, यज्ञेन कल्पन्ताम् । ।। य. 18-1 ।।

vājaśca mē, prasavaśca mē, prayatiśca mē, prasitiśca mē,
dhītiśca mē, kratuśca mē, svaraśca mē, ślōkaśca mē,
śravaśca mē, śrutiśca mē, jyōtiśca mē,
svaśca mē, yajñēna kalpantām

May my prayers be answered,
and may I be granted
- strength,
- creativity,
- endeavor,
- honesty,
- understanding,
- determination,
- strong voice,
- glory,
- patience to listen,
- ability to communicate,
- ability to observe, and lastly
- a place in heaven.

May God make all these wishes come true.

Prayer Seeking Good Life

शं च मे, मयश्च मे, प्रियं च मे, अनुकामश्च मे,
कामश्च मे, सौमनसश्च मे, भगश्च मे, द्रविणं च मे
भद्रं च मे, श्रेयश्च मे, वसीयश्च मे, यशश्च मे
यज्ञेन कल्पन्ताम् । ॥ य. 18-8 ॥

śaṃ ca mē, mayaśca mē, priyaṃ ca mē, anukāmaśca mē,
kāmaśca mē, saumanasaśca mē, bhagaśca mē, draviṇaṃ ca mē
bhadraṃ ca mē, śrēyaśca mē, vasīyaśca mē, yaśaśca mē
yajñēna kalpantām

May my prayers be answered, and
May I be granted
- my welfare and of those I hold dear,
- cheerfulness,
- love,
- grace,
- excellence,
- prosperity, and
- glory.

May God make all these wishes come true.

Adhyāya 19

Prayer Seeking Glory, Courage, Vigor and Zeal

तेजोऽसि तेजो मयि धेहि;
वीर्यमसि वीर्यं मयि धेहि;
बलमसि बलं मयि धेहि;
ओजोऽसि ओजो मयि धेहि;
सहोऽसि सहो मयि धेहि । || य. 19-9 || *

tējō'si tējō mayi dhēhi;
vīryamasi vīryaṃ mayi dhēhi;
balamasi balaṃ mayi dhēhi;
ōjō'si ōjō mayi dhēhi;
sahō'si sahō mayi dhēhi

God!
You are the fountain of glory! Grant me glory.
You are the fountain of courage! Grant me courage.
You are the fountain of power! Grant me power.
You are the fountain of vigor! Grant me vigor.
You are the fountain of zeal! Grant me zeal.

---

* abridged

Faith

व्रतेन दीक्षाम् आप्नोति दीक्षयाप्नोति दक्षिणाम् ।
दक्षिणा श्रद्धाम् आप्नोति श्रद्धया सत्यम् आप्यते ।।
।। य. 19-30 ।।

vratēna dīkṣām āpnōti dīkṣayāpnōti dakṣiṇām
dakṣiṇā śraddhām āpnōti śraddhayā satyam āpyatē

By holy resolve does one obtain consecration.
By consecration does one gain grace.
By grace does one develop trust in God.
Trust in God leads one to the Truth.

Prayer Seeking Purification

पुनन्तु मा देवजनाः पुनन्तु मनसा धियः ।
पुनन्तु विश्वा भूतानि जातवेदः पुनीहि मा ।। य. 19-39 ।।

punantu mā dēvajanāḥ punantu manasā dhiyaḥ
punantu viśvā bhūtāni jātavēdaḥ punīhi mā

O Dēvas!
Please purify me, cleanse my heart and my mind.
Cleanse my whole being. Cleanse the hearts of mankind.

Faith

दृष्ट्वा रूपे व्याकरोत् सत्यानृते प्रजापतिः ।
अश्रद्धामनृतेऽदधात्, श्रद्धां सत्ये प्रजापतिः ।। य. 19-77 ।।

dṛṣṭvā rūpē vyākarōt satyānṛtē prajāpatiḥ
aśraddhāmanṛtē'dadhāt, śraddhāṃ satyē prajāpatiḥ

Viewing both truth and falsehood, God classified the lack of faith in Him to falsehood and faith in Him to truth.

Adhyāya 23

Prayer of Devotion

गणानां त्वा गणपतिꣳ हवामहे,
प्रियाणां त्वा प्रियपतिꣳ हवामहे,
निधीनां त्वा निधिपतिꣳ हवामहे,
वसो मम । आहमजानि गर्भधम्,
आत्वमजासि गर्भधम् । ॥ य. 23-19 ॥

gaṇānāṃ tvā gaṇapatiṃ havāmahē,
priyāṇāṃ tvā priyapatiṃ havāmahē,
nidhīnāṃ tvā nidhipatiṃ havāmahē,
vasō mama . āhamajāni garbhadham,
ātvamajāsi garbhadham

O God! O Gaṇapati!
Among us your subjects, you are our master. Hail to you.
Among the beloved, you are the most beloved. Hail to you.
Among assets, you are the greatest asset. Hail to you.
You live within us and know us from the time we come in the womb.
Yes, since we come in the womb.

Commentary

This is the second prayer composed in the Vēdas, addressing God as Gaṇapati. The first prayer is mantra 2-23-1 of Ṛgvēda Saṃhitā. During the Vedic times Gaṇapati was an epithet of dēva Bṛhaspati. Later Gaṇapati or Gaṇeśa was given a form and parents.

Adhyāya 27

Prayer for the Ruler of the Country

बृहस्पते सवितर् बोधयैनश्ं सश्ंशितं चित् संतराश्ं सश्ं शिशाधि।
वर्धयैनं महते सौभगाय विश्व एनम् अनु मदन्तु देवाः ॥
॥ य. 27-8 ॥

bṛhaspatē savitar bōdhayainaṃ saṃśitaṃ cit santarāṃ saṃśiśādhi
vardhayainaṃ mahatē saubhagāya viśva ēnam anu madantu dēvāḥ

O Bṛhaspati and Savitar! Make our king knowledgeable. Even though he is bright, make his intellect sharper. Exalt him to great heights. Let all Dēvas be pleased with him.

Adhyāya 32

Prayer Singing Glory

तदेवाग्निस् तदादित्यस् तद्वायुस् तद् उ चन्द्रमाः ।
तदेव शुक्रं तद्ब्रह्म ता आपः स प्रजापतिः ।। य. 32-1 ।।

tadēvāgnis tadādityas tadvāyus tad u candramāḥ
tadēva śukraṃ tadbrahma tā āpaḥ sa prajāpatiḥ

God is the fire; He is the wind; He is the waters. He is the sun and moon. His is the splendor. He is the master of all there is.

One God

वेनस् तत् पश्यन् निहितं गुहा सद् यत्र विश्वं भवत्येकनीडम् ।
तस्मिन्निदꣳ सं च वि चैति सर्वꣳ स ओतः प्रोतश् च विभूः
प्रजासु । ।। य. 32-8 ।।

vēnas tat paśyan nihitaṃ guhā sad yatra viśvaṃ bhavatyēkanīḍam
tasminnidaṃ saṃ ca vi caiti sarvaṃ sa ōtaḥ prōtaś ca vibhūḥ prajāsu

The sage beholds the Being who dwells in us all and pervades the entire universe. In that Being is the union of all there is. This Being is the warp and woof of all creatures.

स नो बन्धुर् जनिता स विधाता धामानि वेद भुवनानि विश्वा ।
यत्र देवा अमृतम् आनशानास् तृतीये धामन्नध्यैरयन्त ।।
।। य. 32-10 ।।

sa nō bandhur janitā sa vidhātā dhāmāni vēda bhuvanāni viśvā
yatra dēvā amṛtam ānaśānās tṛtīyē dhāmannadhyairayanta

The Lord is our creator!
He is the cause of everything.
He is our friend.
We know that the whole universe is His abode; and He is imperishable.
By meditating upon Him we obtain immortality.

Prayer Seeking Wisdom

यां मेधां देवगणाः पितरश् चोपासते ।
तया मामद्य मेधयाऽग्ने मेधाविनं कुरु स्वाहा ।। य. 32-14 ।।

yāṃ mēdhāṃ dēvagaṇāḥ pitaraś cōpāsatē
tayā māmadya mēdhayā'gnē mēdhāvinaṃ kuru svāhā

O Wise Lord!

I ask you to sharpen my mind and grant me wisdom — that kind of wisdom which my ancestors and the angels have sought from you.

Adhyāya 34

Prayer Seeking Virtue

येन कर्माण्यपसो मनीषिणो यज्ञे कृण्वन्ति विदथेषु धीराः ।
यद् अपूर्वं यक्षम् अन्तः प्रजानां तन् मे मनः शिव सङ्कल्पम्
अस्तु ।। ।। य. 34-2 ।।

yēna karmāṇyapasō manīṣiṇō yajñē kṛṇvanti vidathēṣu dhīrāḥ
yad apūrvaṃ yakṣam antaḥ prajānāṃ tan mē manaḥ śiva saṅkalpam astu

Inside every human being is a spirited mind; let my spirited mind propel me to noble resolves. Let my actions be like the actions of those active and wise sages who are worthy of emulation.

Prayer Seeking Virtue

यत् प्रज्ञानम् उत चेतो धृतिश्च यज् ज्योतिरन्तर् अमृतं प्रजासु ।
यस्मान्न ऋते किंचन करम क्रियते तन्मे मनः शिवसङ्कल्पम्
अस्तु ।। ।। य. 34-3 ।।

yat prajñānam uta cētō dhṛtiśca yaj jyōtirantar amṛtaṃ prajāsu
yasmānna ṛtē kiṃcana karma kriyatē tanmē manaḥ
śivasaṅkalpam astu

Good actions are possible with the use of stored wisdom, a firm intellect, and the command that comes from the heart, where our soul, the deathless flame, resides.

Let my mind be drawn to noble actions.

सुषारथिर् अश्वानिव यन् मनुष्यान् नेनीयतेऽभीशुभिर् वाजिन इव ।
हृत्प्रतिष्ठं यद् अजिरं जविष्ठं तन् मे मनः शिवसङ्कल्पम् अस्तु ।।
।। य. 34-6 ।।

suṣārathir aśvāniva yan manuṣyān nēnīyatē'bhīśubhir vājina iva
hṛtpratiṣṭhaṃ yad ajiraṃ javiṣṭhaṃ tan mē manaḥ
śivasaṅkalpam astu

A skillful charioteer controls his horses with reins in his hands.

A smart man, likewise, controls himself with the reins of his mind.

Let my swift mind propel me to noble resolves.

Adhyāya 35

Prayer Seeking Good Life

स्योना पृथिवि नो भवानृक्षरा निवेशनी ।
यच्छा नः शर्म सप्रथाः ।
अप नः शोशुचद् अघम् । ।। य. 35-21 ।।

syōnā pṛthivi nō bhavānṛkṣarā nivēśanī
yacchā naḥ śarma saprathāḥ
apa naḥ śōśucad agham

O the Earth! Make yourself a pleasant place for us to settle down. Let our life on earth be troublefree. Let there be no wickedness and injury in our life on this planet.

Adhyāya 36

Prayer Seeking Welfare

शं नो वातः पवताश्ॐ शंनस् तपतु सूर्यः ।
शं नः कनिक्रदद् देवः पर्जन्यो अभिवर्षतु ।। य. 36-10 ।।

śaṃ nō vātaḥ pavatā śaṃnas tapatu sūryaḥ
śaṃ naḥ kanikradad dēvaḥ parjanyō abhivarṣatu

Lord!
Let the breeze be propitious to us;
Let the sun shine for our well-being;
Let the the thunder bring us much needed rain.

Peace Invocation

द्यौः शान्तिर अन्तरिक्षꣳ शान्तिः पृथिवी शान्तिर् आपः
शान्तिर् ओषधयः शान्तिः।
वनस्पतयः शान्तिर् विश्वेदेवाः शान्तिर् ब्रह्म शान्तिः;
सर्वꣳ शान्तिर् एव शान्तिः सा मा शान्तिर् एधि ।।
।। य. 36-17 ।।

dyauḥ śāntira antarikṣaṃ śāntiḥ pṛthivī śāntir āpaḥ śāntir
ōṣadhayaḥ śāntiḥ
vanaspatayaḥ śāntir viśvēdēvāḥ śāntir brahma śāntiḥ
sarvaṃ śāntir ēva śāntiḥ sā mā śāntir ēdhi

May we be in peace and harmony with the heaven, the sky, and the earth;
May we be in harmony with the waters;
May we be in harmony with the plant kingdom;
May we be in harmony with all the Dēvas (divine powers), and, therefore, with God.
May peace and harmony reign everywhere.

Commentary

This verse emphasizes that mankind should not disturb the peace of the earth and the skies by his actions. The man should not pollute the waters, i.e. rivers, lakes, and seas. The man should not destroy the forests or disregard the cultivation of medicinal plants. That the man should do all those things that please God and not do anything that earns the displeasure of God.

A very similar peace invocation is found in Atharvavēda 19-9-14.

Friendliness

दृते दृꣳह मा मित्रस्य मा चक्षुषा सर्वाणि भूतानि समीक्षन्ताम् ।
मित्रस्याहं चक्षुषा सर्वाणि भूतानि समीक्षे ।
मित्रस्य चक्षुषा समीक्षामहे । ।। य. 36-18 ।।

dṛtē dṛṃha mā mitrasya mā cakṣuṣā sarvāṇi bhūtāni samīkṣantām
mitrasyāhaṃ cakṣuṣā sarvāṇi bhūtāni samīkṣē
mitrasya cakṣuṣā samīkṣāmahē

Lord! Make me strong.
May all look on me with the eye of a friend.
May I look on all with the eye of a friend.
May we all be cordial with each other.

Fearlessness

यतो-यतः समीहसे ततो नो अभयं कुरु ।
शं नः कुरु प्रजाभ्योऽभयं नः पशुभ्यः ।। य. 36-22 ।।

yatō-yataḥ samīhasē tatō nō abhayaṅ kuru
śaṃ naḥ kuru prajābhyō'bhayan naḥ paśubhyaḥ

God! Make us fearless by guarding us against whatever troubles could come to us. Give your blessings to our children and security to our animals.

The Goal of Life

तच् चक्षुर् देवहितं पुरस्ताच् छुक्रम् उच्चरत् ।
पश्येम शरदः शतं, जीवेम शरदः शतꣳ
श्रृणुयाम शरदः शतं, प्रब्रवाम शरदः शतम्,
अदीनाः स्याम शरदः शतं, भूयश्च शरदः शतात् ।।
।। य. 36-24 ।।

tac cakṣur dēvahitaṃ purastāc chukram uccarat
paśyēma śaradaḥ śataṃ, jīvēma śaradaḥ śataṃ
śṛṇuyāma śaradaḥ śataṃ, prabravāma śaradaḥ śatam,
adīnāḥ syāma śaradaḥ śataṃ, bhūyaśca śaradaḥ śatāt

God! May we see "The Bright eye" (the sunrise) for a hundred years.

May we be granted
- a hundred years to live;
- a hundred years to see well;
- a hundred years to hear well;
- a hundred years to speak clearly;
- a hundred years of self-dependence;

Yes, all of the above; and even in excess of hundred years.

Adhyāya 37

Prayer Seeking Welfare

पिता नोऽसि पिता नो बोधि नमस्ते अस्तु मा मा हिꣳसीः ।
त्वष्ट्रः मन्तस् त्वा सपेम पुत्रान् पशून् मयि धेहि ।
प्रजाम् अस्मासु धेह्यरिष्टाहꣳ सह पत्या भूयासम् ।। य. 37-20 ।।

pitā nō'si pitā nō bōdhi namastē astu mā mā himṣīḥ
tvaṣṭṛ mantas tvā sapēma putrān paśūn mayi dhēhi
prajām asmāsu dhēhyariṣṭāhaṃ saha patyā bhūyāsam

God! You are our father. Salutations to you.
May my family win your favor.
Grant us children and animals.
Protect my children, my spouse, and me from all harm.

Adhyāya 40

Adhyāya 40 of the Yajurvēda (Vājasanēyī Saṃhitā - Mādhyandina rescension) contains the entire Īśāvāsya Upaniṣad. Please read it in the volume on the Upaniṣads.

III

सामवेद

The Sāmavēda

Prayer Seeking Strength and Victory

एन्द्र पृक्षु कासु चिन् नृम्णं तनूषु धेहि नः ।
सत्राजिद् उग्र पौंस्यम् ।   ।। सा. 231 ।।*

ēndra pṛkṣu kāsu cin nṛmṇaṃ tanūṣu dhēhi naḥ
satrājid ugra pauṃ syam

O Lord! Grant us ever conquering might. In each battle (whether against external foes, or internal foes such as lust, anger, etc.) give us manly strength.

---

* In Sāmavēda Saṃhitā the division of text into chapters is highly unsatisfactory. First the Saṃhitā is divided into two books called Pūrvārcika and Uttarārcika respectively. Pūrvārcika is then divided into Adhyāyas (chapters). Within a chapter groups of ten mantras are formed, each called a daśatī. In Uttarārcika the Adhyāyas start new numbers. Each adhyāya in Uttarārcika is divided into khaṇḍas (segments). Within each khaṇḍa mantra groups are formed based on the author of the mantras. All this leads to enormous difficulty in searching out the location of a mantra. An alternative classification is to number all the mantras of Sāmaveda continuously. This is what has been adopted here.

Prayer of Devotion to One God

समेत विश्वा ओजसा पतिं दिवो य एक इद् भूर् अतिथिर् जनानाम् ।
स पूर्व्यो नूतनम् आजिगीषन्तं वर्तनीर् अनु वावृत एक इत् ।।
।। सा. 372 ।।

samēta viśvā ōjasā patiṃ divō ya ēka id bhūr atithir janānām
sa pūrvyō nūtanam ājigīṣantaṃ vartanīr anu vāvṛta ēka it

Come ye all, with your full grace, to the glorious Lord!

He is the One to whom all pathways turn. He indeed is the One.

Prayer Seeking Glory

यशो मा द्यावा पृथिवी यशो मेन्द्र बृहस्पती ।
यशो भगस्य विन्दतु यशो मा प्रतिमुच्यताम् ।
यशसास्याः संसदोऽहं प्रवदिता स्याम् । ।। सा. 611 ।।

yaśō mā dyāvā pṛthivī yaśō mēndra bṛhaspatī
yaśō bhagasya vindatu yaśō mā pratimucyatām
yaśasāsyāḥ saṃsadō'haṃ pravaditā syām

O Lord! May I receive glory on the earth and in heaven. May Indra, Bṛhaspati, and Bhaga be on my side. May I be blessed with prosperity, and devotion to you. May I carry your message forcefully to fellow human beings. May I, along with this entire congregation, be blessed with everlasting glory.

IV

अथर्ववेद

The Atharvavēda

Kāṇḍa 1

Prayer for Eloquence

ये त्रिषप्ताः परियन्ति विश्वा रूपाणि बिभ्रतः ।
वाचस्पतिर् बला तेषां तन्वो अद्य दधातु मे ।। अ. 1-1-1 ।।*

yē triṣaptāḥ pariyanti viśvā rūpāṇi bibhrataḥ
vācaspatir balā tēṣāṃ tanvō adya dadhātu mē

God has created me from all of the 21 basic items of the universe. May he grant me the gift of eloquence.

Commentary

The word tṛṣaptāḥ in this verse refers to 21 items of which the universe is assumed to be created – five basic elements, five organs of action, five organs of sense, five vital airs (prāṇa, apāna, vyāna, samāna, and udāna), and the individual soul.

---

* In Atharvavēda Saṃhitā the text is arranged in the same fashion as in the Ṛgvēda Saṃhitā. This Saṃhitā is divided into kāṇḍas (chapters). Each kāṇḍa is divided into several sūktas (hymns), and each sūkta consists of several mantras. In the numbering of each mantra the first number refers to the kāṇḍa, the second to the sūkta, and the third to the mantra itself.

Sweet Speech and Behavior

मधुमन् मे निक्रमणं मधुमन् मे परायणम् ।
वाचा वदामि मधुमद् भूयासं मधुसंदृशः ।। अ. 1-34-3 ।।

madhuman mē nikramaṇaṃ madhuman mē parāyaṇam
vācā vadāmi madhumad bhūyāsaṃ madhusandṛśaḥ

Sweet as honey may I begin.
Sweet as honey may I close; and
Sweet as honey may be my entire speech.
May my total being be sweet as honey.

Newly Married Man and Woman to Each Other

मधोर्अस्मि मधुतरो मदुघान् मधुमत्तरः ।
मामित् किल त्वं वनाः शाखां मधुमतीमिव ।। अ. 1-34-4 ।।

madhōrasmi madhutarō madughān madhumattaraḥ
māmit kila tvaṃ vanāḥ śākhāṃ madhumatīmiva

May I be sweeter than honey; sweeter than liquorice.
May you long for me – as a honeybee longs for a flower full of honey.

Kāṇḍa 2

Young Person

स्रक्त्योऽसि प्रतिसरोऽसि प्रत्यभिचरणोऽसि ।
आप्नुहि श्रेयांसमति समं क्राम । ॥ अ. 2-11-2 ॥

sraktyō'si pratisarō'si pratyabhicaraṇō'si
āpnuhi śrēyāṃsamati samaṃ krāma

Listen young person!
You have the dynamism needed for personal growth.
You have the ability to fight with injustice.
Go. Get ahead of your compeers.
God bless.

To Bride and Groom

संचेन् नयाथो अश्विना कामिना सं च वक्षथः ।
सं वां भगासो अग्मत सं चित्तानि समु व्रता ।। अ. 2-30-2 ।।

saṃcēn nayāthō aśvinā kāminā saṃ ca vakṣathaḥ
saṃ vāṃ bhagāsō agmata saṃ cittāni samu vratā

O Bride and Bridegroom!
The angels have united the two of you to make a loving pair.
May you be united in your thoughts and desires;
May you be united in your actions; and
May you toghether achieve glory.

Kāṇḍa 3

Prayer at the Site of New Home

इहैव ध्रुवां नि मिनोमि शालां क्षेमे तिष्ठाति घृतम् उक्षमाणा ।
तां त्वा शाले सर्ववीराः सुवीरा अरिष्टवीरा उप सं चरेम ॥
॥ अ. 3-12-1 ॥

ihaiva dhruvāṃ ni minōmi śālāṃ kṣēmē tiṣṭhāti ghṛtam ukṣamāṇā
tāṃ tvā śālē sarvavīrāḥ suvīrā ariṣṭavīrā upa saṃ carēma

Right here do I erect a firm house.
May it stand on a strong foundation, dripping with prosperity.
May our family, which will live here, consist of brave people.

Prayer at Gṛhapraveśa (House-Warming)

इमा आपः प्र भराम्ययक्ष्मा यक्ष्मनाशनीः ।
गृहानुप प्र सीदाम्यमृतेन सहाग्निना । ।। अ. 3-12-9 ।।

imā āpaḥ pra bharāmyayakṣamā yakṣmanāśanīḥ
gṛhānupa pra sīdāmyamṛtēna sahāgninā

We bring to this house the water which is free from disease and which is curative.

We bring to this house fire immortal.

With these we set our feet in this house and take possession of it.

Prayer for Success in Business

इमामग्ने शरणिं मीमृषो नो यम् अध्वानम् अगाम दूरम् ।
शुनं नो अस्तु प्रपणो विक्रयश्च प्रतिपणः फलिनं मा कृणोतु ।
इदं हव्यं संविदानौ जुषेथां शुनं नो अस्तु चरितम् उत्थितं च ।।
।। अ. 3-15-4 ।।

imāmagnē śaraṇiṃ mīmṛṣō nō yam adhvānam agāma dūram
śunaṃ nō astu prapaṇō vikrayaśca pratipaṇaḥ phalinaṃ mā kṛṇōtu
idaṃ havyaṃ saṃvidānau juṣēthāṃ śunaṃ nō astu caritam utthitaṃ ca

O Lord! It has been a long and hard road.
Please accept our oblations and prayers for the success of our business.
May our purchases and sales be profitable.
May our transactions bring prosperity.

Prayer Seeking Protection

उप त्वा नमसा वयं होतर् वैश्वानर स्तुमः ।
स नः प्रजास्वात्मसु गोषु प्राणेषु जागृहि ।। अ. 3-15-7 ।।

upa tvā namasā vayaṃ hōtar vaiśvānara stumaḥ
sa naḥ prajāsvātmasu gōṣu prāṇēṣu jāgṛhi

O Lord! You are the protector.
We bring our adoration and reverence to you.
Guard our lives and those of our children.
Protect our animals.

Love and Unity : The Sāmmanasya Sūkta

सहृदयं सां मनस्यम् अविद्वेषं कृणोमि वः ।
अन्यो अन्यम् अभि हर्यत वत्सं जातम् इवाघ्न्या ।।
।। अ. 3-30-1 ।।

sahṛdayaṃ sāṃ manasyam avidvēṣaṃ kṛṇōmi vaḥ
anyō anyam abhi haryata vatsaṃ jātam ivāghnyā

God Said, "I want you to be of one heart and one mind, devoid of hate. Love one another as the cow loves her newborn calf."

Love and Unity

अनुव्रतः पितुः पुत्रो मात्रा भवतु संमनाः ।
जाया पत्ये मधुमतीं वाचं वदतु शन्तिवाम् ।। अ. 3-30-2 ।।

anuvrataḥ pituḥ putrō mātrā bhavatu sammanāḥ
jāyā patyē madhumatīṃ vācaṃ vadatu śantivām

Let the son be devoted to his father.
Let him be of one mind with his mother.
Let the wife be sweet and gentle to her husband.

मा भ्राता भ्रातरं द्विक्षन्मा स्वसारम् उत स्वसा ।
सम्यञ्चः सव्रता भूत्वा वाचं वदत भद्रया ।। अ. 3-30-3 ।।

mā bhrātā bhrātaraṃ dvikṣanmā svasāram uta svasā
samyañcaḥ savratā bhūtvā vācaṃ vadata bhadrayā

Let brother not hate brother.
Let sister not hate sister.
Let the family-members be united in heart, be of one goal, and speak sweetly with each other.

Harmony in the Family

येन देवा न वियन्ति नो च विद्विषते मिथः ।
तत् कृण्मो ब्रह्म वो गृहे संज्ञानं पुरुषेभ्यः ।। अ. 3-30-4 ।।

yēna dēvā na viyanti nō ca vidviṣatē mithaḥ
tat kṛṇmō brahma vō gṛhē sañjñānaṃ puruṣēbhyaḥ

The Lord said, "I grant the same enlightenment to your family as the Dēvas have, among whom there is no discord".

Unity and Togetherness

ज्यायस्वन्तश् चित्तिनो मा वि यौष्ट संराधयन्तः सधुराश्
चरन्तः ।
अन्यो अन्यस्मै वल्गु वदन्त एत सध्रीचीनान् वः संमनसस्
कृणोमि । ।। अ. 3-30-5 ।।

jyāyasvantaś cittinō mā vi yauṣṭa saṃrādhayantaḥ sadhurāś carantaḥ
anyō anyasmai valgu vadanta ēta sadhrīcīnān vaḥ sammanasas kṛṇōmi

In working with others, may we follow the example of our elders, and work in co-operation and with discipline.

May we be united in resolve, and pleasant in communication.

Praying Together

समानी प्रपा सह वोऽन्नभागः समाने योक्त्रे सह वो युनज्मि ।
सम्यञ्चोऽग्नि सपर्यतारा नाभिम् इवाभितः ।। अ. 3-30-6 ।।

samānī prapā saha vō'nnabhāgaḥ samānē yōktrē saha vō yunajmi
samyañcō'gni saparyatārā nābhim ivābhitaḥ

May we assemble, for the worship of the Lord, to pray together, like spokes around the hub of a wheel.

May we eat and drink together.

Following Your Leader

सध्रीचीनान् वः संमनसस् कृणोम्येकश्नुष्टीन्त्संवननेन सर्वान् ।
देवा इवामृतं रक्षमाणाः सायंप्रातः सौमनसो वो अस्तु ।।
।। अ. 3-30-7 ।।

sadhrīcīnān vaḥ saṃmanasas
kṛṇōmyēkaśnuṣṭīntsaṃvananēna sarvān
dēvā ivāmṛtaṃ rakṣamāṇāḥ sāyamprātaḥ saumanasō vō astu

The Lord Spoke, "I render you of common goal, and of united mind. Follow your chosen leader. Let the immortal Dēvas protect you, and may you be happy night and day."

Kāṇḍa 4

The Omnipresent God

यस् तिष्ठति चरति यश् च वञ्चति यो निलायं चरति यः प्रतङ्कम् ।
द्वौ सं निषद्य यन् मन्त्रयेते राजा तद् वेद वरुणस् तृतीयः ।।
।। अ. 4-16-2 ।।

yas tiṣṭhati carati yaś ca vañcati yō nilāyaṃ carati yaḥ prataṅkam
dvau saṃ niṣadya yan mantrayētē rājā tad vēda varuṇas tṛtīyaḥ

Whether two men are sitting down or moving, doing things in secret, or whispering, they should remember that there is always that third One present - the omnipresent ruler of the world.

उतेयं भूमिर् वरुणस्य राज्ञ उतासौ द्यौर् बृहती दूरेअन्ता ।
उतो समुद्रौ वरुणस्य कुक्षी उतास्मिन्नल्प उदके निलीनः ।।
।। अ. 4-16-3 ।।

utēyaṃ bhūmir varuṇasya rājña utāsau dyaur bṛhatī dūrēantā
utō samudrau varuṇasya kukṣī utāsminnalpa udakē nilīnaḥ

The empire of the King of the earth and the boundless skies is, far-flung. The two mighty oceans are his loins and yet He resides in a tiny drop of water.

Recognition of God

यः समाम्यो ३ वरुणो यो व्याम्यो ३
यः संदेश्यो ३ वरुणो यो विदेश्यः ।
यो दैवो वरुणो यश्च मानुषः । || अ. 4-16-8 ||

yaḥ samāmyō 3 varuṇō yō vyāmyō 3
yaḥ sandēśyō 3 varuṇō yō vidēśyaḥ
yō daivō varuṇō yaśca mānuṣaḥ

God is divine, yet He is also human.
God is, from whom everything emerges, and
God is, to whom everything goes back.
God is our friend and yet, men do not know Him.

Kāṇḍa 5

Prayer by the Priest

सविता प्रसवानाम् अधिपतिः स मावतु ।
अस्मिन् ब्रह्मण्यस्मिन् कर्मण्यस्यां
पुरोधायाम् अस्यां प्रतिष्ठायाम्
अस्यां चित्त्याम् अस्याम् आकूत्याम्
अस्याम् आशिष्यस्यां देवहूत्यां स्वाहा । ।। अ. 5-24-1 ।।

savitā prasavānām adhipatiḥ sa māvatu
asmin brahmaṇyasmin karmaṇyasyāṃ
purōdhāyām asyāṃ pratiṣṭhāyām
asyāṃ cittyām asyām ākūtyām
asyām āśiṣyasyāṃ dēvahūtyāṃ svāhā

O God! the giver of life to us all! You are my master!

When I am praying;
When I am discharging my duties;
When I am performing my priestly functions;
When I am deep in thought;
When I am in the process of defining my purposes;
When I am in the company of learned people;

in all these situations please protect me (by showing me the right direction)

Kāṇḍa 6

Prayer Seeking Fearlessness

अभयं द्यावापृथिवी इहास्तु नोऽभयं सोमः सविता नः कृणोतु ।
अभयं नोऽस्तूर्वन्तरिक्षं सप्तऋषीणां च हविषाभयं नो अस्तु ।।
।। अ. 6-40-1 ।।

abhayaṃ dyāvāpṛthivī ihāstu nō'bhayaṃ sōmaḥ savitā naḥ kṛṇōtu
abhayaṃ nō'stūrvantarikṣaṃ saptarṣīṇāṃ ca haviṣābhayaṃ nō astu

May the Earth and the Heaven grant us fearlessness.
May the boundless space breathe fearlessness in us.
May the Saptarṣi (the seven stars of the Great Bear) breathe fearlessness in us.

Prayer Seeking Intellect

मयि वर्चो अथो यशोऽथो यज्ञस्य यत् पयः ।
तन्मयि प्रजापतिर् दिवि द्याम् इव दृंहतु ।। अ. 6-69-3 ।।

mayi varcō athō yaśō'thō yajñasya yat payaḥ
tanmayi prajāpatir divi dyām iva dṛṃhatu

Just as the Lord has firmly established the bright sun in the sky, may He establish the brightness of intellect in me.

May I earn glory from good actions.

Sweet Speech

अश्विना सारघेण मा मधुनाङ्क्तं शुभस्पती ।
यथा भर्गस्वतीं वाचम् आवदानि जनाँ अनु ।। अ. 6-69-2 ।।

aśvinā sāraghēṇa mā madhunāṅktaṃ śubhaspatī
yathā bhargasvatīṃ vācam āvadāni janāṁ anu

Auspicious Aśvins! The true reality!

May my speech be as sweet as honey, so that I may convey your glorious message to mankind in a pleasing manner.

Blessings to Bride and Bridegroom

संज्ञपनं वो मनसोऽथो संज्ञपनं हृदः ।
अथो भगस्य यच् छ्रान्तं तेन संज्ञपयामि वः ।।
।। अ. 6-74-2 ।।

sañṃjñapanaṃ vō manasō'thō saṃjñapanaṃ hṛdaḥ
athō bhagasya yac chrāntaṃ tēna sañjñapayāmi vaḥ

May you have the harmony of mind and heart. May the Lord cause you to pursue common goals.

त्वष्टा जायाम् अजनयत् त्वष्टास्यै त्वां पतिम् ।
त्वष्टा सहस्रम् आयूंषि दीर्घम् आयुः कृणोतु वाम् ।। अ. 6-78-3 ।।

tvaṣṭā jāyām ajanayat tvaṣṭāsyai tvāṃ patim
tvaṣṭā sahasram āyūṃṣi dīrgham āyuḥ kṛṇōtu vām

The Lord has made her for you and the Lord has created you for her. May He grant long life to both of you.

Prayer Seeking Forgiveness.

यद् अन्तरिक्षं पृथिवीम् उत द्यां यन् मातरं पितरं वा जिहिंसिम ।
अयं तस्माद् गार्हपत्यो नो अग्निर् उदिन्नयाति सुकृतस्य लोकम् ।।
।। अ. 6-120-1 ।।

yad antarikṣaṃ pṛthivīm uta dyāṃ yan mātaraṃ pitaraṃ vā jihiṃsima
ayaṃ tasmād gārhapatyō nō agnir udinnayāti sukṛtasya lōkam

If we have done wrong to the earth, the space, or the heavens; or, if we have offended our mother or father - may the good Lord forgive us and guide us to perform good deeds.

Prayer by the Newlyweds

य इमां देवो मेखलाम् आबबन्ध यः संननाह य उ नो युयोज ।
यस्य देवस्य प्रशिषा चरामः स पारम् इच्छात् स उ नो विमुञ्चात् ॥ ॥ अ. 6-133-1 ॥

ya imāṃ dēvō mēkhalām ābabandha yaḥ sannanāha ya u nō yuyōja
yasya dēvasya praśiṣā carāmaḥ sa pāram icchāt sa u nō vimuñcāt

The Almighty Lord has yoked us together in a strong bond. He is the one whose will prevails. May He keep us free (from troubles) through the end of our days.

Kāṇḍa 7

The Unity of Thought & Action

प्रजापतिर् जनयति प्रजा इमा धाता दधातु सुमनस्यमानः ।
सं जानानाः संमनसः सयोनयो मयि पुष्टं पुष्टपतिर् दधातु ।।
।। अ. 7-19-1 ।।

prajāpatir janayati prajā imā dhātā dadhātu sumanasyamānaḥ
saṃ jānānāḥ sammanasaḥ sayōnayō mayi puṣṭaṃ puṣṭapatir dadhātu

God is our lord and master. He is our parent and well-wisher. He is our support. He wants us to acquire wisdom and unity among ourselves. Unanimity of thought and action in our society will make us strong.

Statement by the Newlyweds

अक्ष्यौ नौ मधुसङ्काशे अनीकं नौ समञ्जनम् ।
अन्तः कृणुष्व मां हृदि मन इन्नौ सहासति ।। अ. 7-36-1 ।।

akṣyau nau madhusaṅkāśē anīkaṃ nau samañjanam
antaḥ kṛṇuṣva māṃ hṛdi mana innau sahāsati

Sweet like honey be the messages we convey to each other with our glances.

May we place each other in our hearts; and
May our minds become one.

Woman to Man at the Wedding Ceremony

अभि त्वा मनुजातेन दधामि मम वाससा ।
यथासो मम केवलो नान्यासां कीर्तयाश्चन ।। अ. 7-37-1 ।।

abhi tvā manujātēna dadhāmi mama vāsasā
yathāsō mama kēvalō nānyāsāṃ kīrtayāścana

I envelope thee in my garment, and declare that thou shalt be mine and mine alone.

Even the thought of other women should not enter your mind.

Man and Woman to Each other Immediately After the Wedding Ceremony.

शं नो वातो वातु शं नस् तपतु सूर्यः ।
अहानि शं भवन्तु नः शं रात्री प्रति धीयतां शम् उषा नो व्युच्छतु ।।
।। अ. 7-69-1 ।।

śaṃ nō vātō vātu śaṃ nas tapatu sūryaḥ ahāni śaṃ bhavantu naḥ śaṃ rātrī prati dhīyatāṃ śam uṣā nō vyucchatu

May the wind bring to us joy.
May the sunshine fill joy in us.
May our days be filled with joy.
May the nights be gifts of peace.
May the sunrise bring us joy.

Kāṇḍa 8

Blessing to a Younger Person

तुभ्यं वातः पवतां मातरिश्वा तुभ्यं वर्षन् त्वमृतान्यापः ।
सूर्यस् ते तन्वे३ शं तपाति त्वां मृत्युर् दयतां मा प्र मेष्ठाः ।।
।। अ. 8-1-5 ।।

tubhyaṃ vātaḥ pavatāṃ mātariśvā tubhyaṃ varṣan tvamṛtānyāpaḥ
sūryas tē tanvē3 śaṃ tapāti tvāṃ mṛtyur dayatāṃ mā pra mēṣṭhāḥ

May the wind purify you;
May the waters bring you immortality;
May the warmth of the sun bless your bodies;
May death spare you so that you may live long.

Blessing to a Younger Person

उद्यानं ते पुरुष नावयानं जीवातुं ते दक्षतातिं कृणोमि ।
आ हि रोहेमम् अमृतं सुखं रथम् अथ जिर्विर् विदथमा
वदासि ।। ।। अ. 8-1-6 ।।

udyānaṃ tē puruṣa nāvayānaṃ jīvātuṃ tē dakṣatātiṃ kṛṇōmi
ā hi rōhēmam amṛtaṃ sukhaṃ rathamatha jirvir
vidathamāvidathamā vadāsi

May you rise and not fall.
May you be granted long life.
May you achieve success in your occupation.
May you ride the chariot of happiness;
May you grow in wisdom with years.

Blessing to a Younger Person

शिवे ते स्तां द्यावापृथिवी असंतापे अभिश्रियौ शं ते सूर्य आ तपतु
शं वातो वातु ते हृदे ।
शिवा अभि क्षरन्तु त्वापो दिव्याः पयस्वतीः ।। अ. 8-2-14 ।।

śivē tē stāṃ dyāvāpṛthivī asaṃtāpē abhiśriyau śaṃ tē sūrya
ā tapatu śaṃ vātō vātu tē hṛdē
śivā abhi kṣarantu tvāpō divyāḥ payasvatīḥ

May the Earth and the Heaven be auspicious and troublefree for you.
May the sunshine bring you blessings.
May the wind bring you good luck; and
May the rivers bring you plenty of clear water for your good.

Kāṇḍa 9

The Power of Love

यावती द्यावापृथिवी वरिम्णा यावद् आपः सिष्यदुर् यावद् अग्निः ।
ततस् त्वम् असि ज्यायान् विश्वहा महांस् तस्मै ते काम नम इत् कृणोमि ।। ।। अ. 9-2-20 ।।

न वै वातश् च न कामम् आप्नोति नाग्निः सूर्यो नोत चन्द्रमाः ।
ततस् त्वम् असि ज्यायान् विश्वहा
महांस् तस्मै ते काम नम इत् कृणोमि ।। ।। अ. 9-2-24 ।।

yāvatī dyāvāpṛthivī varimṇā yāvad āpaḥ siṣyadur yāvad agniḥ
tatas tvam asi jyāyān viśvahā mahāṃs tasmai tē kāma nama it kṛṇōmi

na vai vātaś ca na kāmam āpnōti nāgniḥ sūryō nōta candramāḥ
tatas tvam asi jyāyān viśvahā
mahāṃs tasmai tē kāma nama it kṛṇōmi

You, O Love, are greater than all.
You are higher than heaven, and wider than earth.
You, O Love, are greater than all.
You are swifter than wind, and hotter than fire.
You, O Love, are greater than all.

Prayer for the House and the Family

प्राच्या दिशः शालाया नमो महिम्ने स्वाहा देवेभ्यः स्वाह्येभ्यः ।।
दक्षिणाया दिशः शालाया नमो महिम्ने स्वाहा देवेभ्यः स्वाह्येभ्यः ।।
प्रतीच्या दिशः शालाया नमो महिम्ने स्वाहा देवेभ्यः स्वाह्येभ्यः ।।
उदीच्या दिशः शालाया नमो महिम्ने स्वाहा देवेभ्यः स्वाह्येभ्यः ।।
ध्रुवाया दिशः शालाया नमो महिम्ने स्वाहा देवेभ्यः स्वाह्येभ्यः ।।
ऊर्ध्वाया दिशः शालाया नमो महिम्ने स्वाहा देवेभ्यः स्वाह्येभ्यः ।।
दिशोदिशः शालाया नमो महिम्ने स्वाहा देवेभ्यः स्वाह्येभ्यः ।।
।। अ. 9-3-25/31 ।।

prācyā diśaḥ śālāyā namō mahimnē svāhā dēvēbhyaḥ svāhyēbhyaḥ
dakṣiṇāyā diśaḥ śālāyā namō mahimnē svāhā dēvēbhyaḥ svāhyēbhyaḥ
pratīcyā diśaḥ śālāyā namō mahimnē svāhā dēvēbhyaḥ svāhyēbhyaḥ
udīcyā diśaḥ śālāyā namō mahimnē svāhā dēvēbhyaḥ svāhyēbhyaḥ
dhruvāyā diśaḥ śālāyā namō mahimnē svāhā dēvēbhyaḥ svāhyēbhyaḥ
ūrdhvāyā diśaḥ śālāyā namō mahimnē svāhā dēvēbhyaḥ svāhyēbhyaḥ
diśōdiśaḥ śālāyā namō mahimnē svāhā dēvēbhyaḥ svāhyēbhyaḥ

From the eastern direction,
From the southern direction,
From the western direction,
From the northern direction,
From the depths below,
From the heights above,
I summon a blessing, to the glory of this house.
Praise be to God, the praiseworthy, forever and ever.

To the Widow

या पूर्वं पतिं वित्त्वाथान्यं विन्दतेऽपरम् ।
पञ्चौदनं च तावजं ददातो न वि योषतः ।। अ. 9-5-27 ।।

yā pūrvaṃ patiṃ vittvāthānyaṃ vindatē'param
pañcaudanaṃ ca tāvajaṃ dadātō na vi yōṣataḥ

A woman may lose her husband to death.

Such a woman may find a new husband and dedicate her love to the newlyfound mate.

Commentary

In Vedic times widow remarriage was encouraged.

Kāṇḍa 10

Glory of God

यस्मिन् भूमिर् अन्तरिक्षं द्यौर् यस्मिन्न् अध्याहिता ।
यत्राग्निश् चन्द्रमाः सूर्यो वातस् तिष्ठन्त्यार्पिताः स्कम्भं तं
ब्रूहि कतमः स्विदेव सः ।। ।। अ. 10-7-12 ।।

yasmin bhūmir antarikṣaṃ dyaur yasminn adhyāhitā
yatrāgniś candramāḥ sūryō vātas tiṣṭhantyārpitāḥ skambhaṃ
taṃ brūhi katamaḥ svidēva saḥ

Would someone teach me about the One Lord in whom the earth, the skies, and the heaven subsist; and who is the support of the sun, the moon, the fire, and the wind?

Prayer Singing Glory

यो भूतं च भव्यं च सर्वं यश् चाधितिष्ठति ।
स्वर् यस्य च केवलं तस्मै ज्येष्ठाय ब्रह्मणे नमः ।। अ. 10-8-1 ।।

yō bhūtaṃ ca bhavyaṃ ca sarvaṃ yaś cādhitiṣṭhati
svar yasya ca kēvalaṃ tasmai jyēṣṭhāya brahmaṇē namaḥ

We pay our homage to Him and Him only — the glorious Lord to whom the entire past belonged and to whom belongs the entire future.

Recognition of God

त्वं स्त्री त्वं पुमान् असि त्वं कुमार उत वा कुमारी ।
त्वं जीर्णो दण्डेन वञ्चसि त्वं जातो भवसि विश्वतोमुखः ।।
।। अ. 10-8-27 ।।

tvaṃ strī tvaṃ pumān asi tvaṃ kumāra uta vā kumārī
tvaṃ jīrṇō daṇḍēna vañcasi tvaṃ jātō bhavasi viśvatōmukhaḥ

Lord!
You are (in) the man;
you are (in) the woman;
you are (in) the child;
you are (in) the old person;
you exist in all of us, and you exist everywhere.

Kāṇḍa 11

Prayer Singing Glory

नमः सायं नमः प्रातर् नमो रात्र्या नमो दिवा ।
भवाय च शर्वाय चोभाभ्याम् अकरं नमः ।। अ. 11-2-16 ।।

namaḥ sāyaṃ namaḥ prātar namō rātryā namō divā
bhavāya ca śarvāya cōbhābhyām akaraṃ namaḥ

Let us pay our homage in the morning, during the day, in the evening, and during the night, to the Lord who grants us life and who also takes it away.

तस्माद् वै विद्वान् पुरुषम् इदं ब्रह्मेति मन्यते ।
सर्वा ह्यस्मिन् देवता गावो गोष्ठ इवासते ।। अ. 11-8-32 ।।

tasmād vai vidvān puruṣam idaṃ brahmēti manyatē
sarvā hyasmin dēvatā gāvō gōṣṭha ivāsatē

Wise people know that human body is a temple of God. All the Dēvas live inside the human body just as cows live in the cowshed.

Kāṇḍa 12

Our Motherland

सत्यं बृहद् ऋतम् उग्रं दीक्षा तपो ब्रह्म यज्ञः पृथिवीं धारयन्ति ।
सा नो भूतस्य भव्यस्य पत्न्युरुं लोकं पृथिवी नः कृणोतु ।।
।। अ. 12-1-1 ।।

satyaṃ bṛhad ṛtam ugraṃ dīkṣā tapō brahma yajñaḥ pṛthivīṃ dhārayanti
sā nō bhūtasya bhavyasya patnyuruṃ lōkaṃ pṛthivī naḥ kṛṇōtu

The qualities of truthfulness, righteousness, daring, and hard work, combined with belief in God, prayer, and charity, are what upholds a nation.

May our country, the mistress of our past, present, and future, open wide opportunities for us.

God's Generosity and Mercy

गिरयस् ते परवता हिमवन्तोऽरण्यं ते पृथिवि स्योनम् अस्तु ।
बभ्रुं कृष्णां रोहिणीं विश्वरूपां ध्रुवां भूमिं पृथिवीम् इन्द्रगुप्ताम् ।
अजीतोऽहतो अक्षतोऽध्यष्ठां पृथिवीम् अहम् ।।
।। अ. 12-1-11 ।।

girayas tē parvatā himavantō'raṇyaṃ tē pṛthivi syōnam astu
babhruṃ kṛṣṇāṃ rōhiṇīṃ viśvarūpāṃ dhruvāṃ bhūmiṃ pṛthivīm indraguptām
ajītō'hatō akṣatō'dhyaṣṭhāṃ pṛthivīm aham

On this majestic earth with hills and snow-capped mountains, with forests and rivers running blue waters, with black, brown, and red soils that sustain us, do I walk under the protection of the Lord, unslain, unwounded, undefeated.

Friendliness and Strength

जनं बिभ्रती बहुधा विवाचसं नानाधर्माणं पृथिवी यथौकसम् ।
सहस्रं धारा द्रविणस्य मे दुहां ध्रुवेव धेनुरनपस्फुरन्ती ।।
।। अ. 12-1-45 ।।

janaṃ bibhratī bahudhā vivācasaṃ nānādharmāṇaṃ pṛthivī yathaukasam
sahasraṃ dhārā draviṇasya mē duhāṃ dhruvēva dhēnuranapasphurantī

May the Earth that bears people speaking varied languages, with various religious rites according to places of abode, enrich me with wealth in a thousand streams, like a milch cow that never fails.

Commentary

The verse acknowledges that the earth belongs to different races, speaking different languages and following different religions. This is a commitment for mutual respect.

Friendliness and Strength

यद् वदामि मधुमत् तद् वदामि यद् ईक्षे तद् वनन्ति मा ।
त्विषीमान् अस्मि जूतिमान् अवान्यान् हन्मि दोधतः ।।
।। अ. 12-1-58 ।।

yad vadāmi madhumat tad vadāmi yad īkṣē tad vananti mā
tviṣīmān asmi jūtimān avānyān hanmi dōdhataḥ

I look at people with friendliness, and I talk to them cordially. They do the same to me.

Yet, I am strong and energetic enough to thwart the attempts of those who are unfriendly and who want to hurt me.

Statement by Bride and Bridegroom at the Wedding Ceremony

स्वर्गं लोकम् अभि नो नयासि सं जायया सह पुत्रैः स्याम ।
गृह्णामि हस्तम् अनु मैत्वत्र मा नस् तारीन् निर्ऋतिर् मो
अरातिः ।। ।। अ. 12-3-17 ।।

svargaṃ lōkam abhi nō nayāsi saṃ jāyayā saha putraiḥ syāma
gṛhṇāmi hastam anu maitvatra mā nas tārīn nirṛtir mō arātiḥ

I am accepting the hand of my life-partner today.
Lord, lead us to the world of supreme bliss and joy,
where I could live with my family;
where adversity and destruction may not follow us.

Kāṇḍa 13

Human Body - The Temple of God

य इमे द्यावापृथिवी जजान यो द्रापिं कृत्वा भुवनामि वस्ते।
।। अ. 13-3-1 ।।

ya imē dyāvāpṛthivī jajāna yō drāpiṃ kṛtvā bhuvanāmi vastē

God created the heaven, the earth, and the man, and then entered the body of the man.

One God

तम् इदं निगतं सहः स एष एक एक वृद् एक एव ।
एते अस्मिन् देवा एक वृतो भवन्ति ।। अ. 13-4-12/13 ।।

tam idaṃ nigataṃ sahaḥ sa ēṣa ēka ēka vṛd ēka ēva
ētē asmin dēvā ēka vṛtō bhavanti

God is almighty. He is the One and only.
In Him all the Dēvas become unified.

One God

नाष्टमो न नवमो दशमो नाप्युच्यते ।
न पञ्चमो न षष्ठः सप्तमो नाप्युच्यते ।
न द्वितीयो न तृतीयश् चतुर्थो नाप्युच्यते ।
य एतं देवम् एकवृतं वेद ।
सर्वे अस्मिन् देवा एक वृतो भवन्ति ।
स सर्वस्मै वि पश्यति यच्च प्राणति यच्च न ।
तम् इदं निगतं सहः स एष एक एकवृद् एक एव ।
।। अ. 13-4-15/21 ।।*

nāṣṭamō na navamō daśamō nāpyucyatē
na pañcamō na ṣaṣṭhaḥ saptamō nāpyucyatē
na dvitīyō na tṛtīyaś caturthō nāpyucyatē
ya ētaṃ dēvam ēkavṛtaṃ vēda
sarvē asmin dēvā ēka vṛtō bhavanti
sa sarvasmai vi paśyati yacca prāṇati yacca na
tam idaṃ nigataṃ sahaḥ sa ēṣa ēka ēkavṛd ēka ēva

There are no eight, nine, or ten Gods;
there are no five, six, or seven Gods;
there are not even two, three, or four Gods;
To him who knows, there is only one God.
All deities are but different names of the One.
He is the One, the only One.
He is the One who oversees what breathes and what does not breathe.
He is the One with all the power and the authority.

---

* rearranged

Kāṇḍa 14

Blessing to the Bride

आशासाना सौमनसं प्रजां सौभाग्यं रयिम्।
पत्युर् अनुव्रता भूत्वा सं नह्यस्वामृताय कम्।। अ. 14-1-42 ।।

āśāsānā saumanasaṃ prajāṃ saubhāgyaṃ rayim
patyur anuvratā bhūtvā saṃ nahyasvāmṛtāya kam

O Bride!

May your wishes for happiness, for children, for financial well-being, and for being blessed, be fulfilled.

Go. Get busy merging your mind with that of your husband; and may both of you live long.

Statement by Priest or Elder at the Wedding Ceremony

इहेमाव् इन्द्र सं नुद चक्रवाकेव दम्पती ।
प्रजयैनौ स्वस्तकौ विश्वम् आयुर् व्यश्नुताम् ।। अ. 14-2-64 ।।

ihēmāv indra saṃ nuda cakravākēva dampatī
prajayainau svastakau viśvam āyur vyaśnutām

O Lord!

Unite this man and this woman in love like a pair of cakravāka love-birds.

May this couple be blessed with children; and

May both be blessed to enjoy the full span of life.

Man to Woman

अमोऽहम् अस्मि सा त्वं, सामाहम् अस्मि ऋक् त्वं, द्यौर् अहं पृथिवी त्वम् ।
ताविह सं भवाव, प्रजाम् आ जनयावहै ।। अ. 14-2-71 ।।

amō'ham asmi sā tvaṃ, sāmāham asmi ṛk tvaṃ, dyaur ahaṃ pṛthivī tvam
tāviha saṃ bhavāva, prajām ā janayāvahai

I am the man; you are the woman
I am the song; you are the lyric
I am the sky; you are the earth
We two shall make a home;
And, We will bring forth children.

Kāṇḍa 19

Peace Invocation

पृथिवी शान्तिर् अन्तरिक्षं शान्तिर् द्यौः शान्तिर आपः शान्तिर्
ओषधयः शान्तिर वनस्पतयः शान्तिर्
विश्वे मे देवाः शान्तिः सर्वे मे देवाः शान्तिः
शान्तिः शान्तिः शान्तिभिः ।
ताभिः शान्तिभिः सर्व शान्तिभिः
शमयामोऽहं यदिह घोरं
यदिह क्रूरं यदिह पापं
तच्छान्तं तच्छिवं सर्वमेव शमस्तु नः ।। अ. 19-9-14 ।।

pṛthivī śāntir antarikṣaṃ śāntir dyauḥ śāntira āpaḥ śāntir
ōṣadhayaḥ śāntira vanaspatayaḥ śāntir
viśvē mē dēvāḥ śāntiḥ sarvē mē dēvāḥ śāntiḥ
śāntiḥ śāntiḥ śāntibhiḥ
tābhiḥ śāntibhiḥ sarva śāntibhiḥ
śamayāmō'haṃ yadiha ghōraṃ
yadiha krūraṃ yadiha pāpaṃ
tacchāntaṃ tacchivaṃ sarvamēva śamastu naḥ

Let us be in peace and harmony with our earth and with the skies.
Let us be in harmony with the waters and with the plant kingdom;
Let us be in harmony with the forests.
Let us be in peace and harmony with the Dēvas.
May we dedicate this invocation for harmony everywhere.

May the Lord make a gift of peace to us and to all men.
May harmony be established by removing what is dreadful.
May harmony be established by removing what is sinful.
May peace and harmony reign everywhere.

Commentary

This is the first ever promise of man to live in harmony with the earth and its environs. This promise has been broken by polluting the earth, the waters, and the air. It has been broken by wiping out the forests and by producing harmful plants such as tobacco and marijuana. Peace is being repeatedly destroyed by dreadful and sinful actions of mankind. The wish of our sages for peace and harmony everywhere can be obtained only by fulfilling the promises made in this great invocation.

Prayer Seeking Fearlessness

अभयं नः करत्यन्तरिक्षम् अभयं द्यावापृथिवी उभे इमे ।
अभयं पश्चाद् अभयं पुरस्ताद् उत्तराद् अधराद् अभयं नो अस्तु ।।
।। अ. 19-15-5 ।।

abhayaṃ naḥ karatyantarikṣam abhayaṃ dyāvāpṛthivī ubhē imē
abhayaṃ paścād abhayaṃ purastād uttarād adharād abhayaṃ nō astu

May the skies make us fearless.
May the earth make us fearless.
May the heaven make us fearless.
May fearlessness envelope us from the front, from behind, from below, and from up above.

Prayer Seeking Fearlessness

अभयं मित्राद् अभयम् अमित्राद् अभयं ज्ञाताद् अभयं पुरो यः ।
अभयं नक्तम् अभयं दिवा नः सर्वा आशा मम मित्रं भवन्तु ।।
।। अ. 19-15-6 ।।

abhayaṃ mitrād abhayam amitrād abhayaṃ jñātād abhayaṃ purō yaḥ
abhayaṃ naktam abhayaṃ divā naḥ sarvā āśā mama mitraṃ bhavantu

May I be fearless of the friend, fearless of the foe, fearless of the known, and fearless of the unknown.

May my days be without fear and my nights be without fear.

Let the whole world desire to be friendly with me.

Prayer Seeking Healthy Long Life

वाङ्म आसन् नसोः प्राणश् चक्षुर् अक्ष्णोः श्रोत्रं कर्णयोः ।
अपलिताः केशा अशोणा दन्ता बहु बाह्वोर् बलम् ।।
।। अ. 19-60-1 ।।

ऊर्वोर् ओजो जङ्घयोर् जवः पादयोः ।
प्रतिष्ठा अरिष्टानि मे सर्वात्मानिभृष्टः ।। अ. 19-60-2 ।।

vāṅma āsan nasōḥ prāṇaś cakṣur akṣaṇōḥ śrōtraṃ karṇayōḥ
apalitāḥ kēśā aśōṇā dantā bahu bāhvōr balam

ūrvōr ōjō jaṅghayōr javaḥ pādayōḥ
pratiṣṭhā ariṣṭāni mē sarvātmānibhṛṣṭaḥ

O Lord! So long as I breathe
May my voice remain clear;
May my sight remain unimpaired;
My my hearing remain intact;
May my hair not turn gray;
May my teeth remain white;
May my arms remain strong;
May my thighs remain powerful;
May my legs remain strong;
May my feet remain stable;
May all of my limbs remain intact;
May my soul ever remain untainted.

Prayer Seeking Long Life

जीवेम शरदः शतम् ।
पश्येम शरदः शतम् ।
बुध्येम शरदः शतम् ।
रोहेम शरदः शतम् ।
पूषेम शरदः शतम् ।
भवेम शरदः शतम् ।
भूयेम शरदः शतम् ।
भूयसीः शरदः शतात् । ।। अ. 19-67-1/8 ।। *

jīvēma śaradaḥ śatam
paśyēma śaradaḥ śatam
budhyēma śaradaḥ śatam
rōhēma śaradaḥ śatam
pūṣēma śaradaḥ śatam
bhavēma śaradaḥ śatam
bhūyēma śaradaḥ śatam
bhūyasīḥ śaradaḥ śatāt

May I live a hundred summers.
May I retain my eyesight a hundred summers.
May I retain my mental faculty a hundred summers.
May my wisdom continue to grow a hundred summers.
May I retain my strength a hundred summers.
May I remain pure and sinless a hundred summers.
Yes, May I achieve all of the above for even more than a hundred summers.

---

* rearranged

The Subjectwise Arrangement of the Four Vēdas

Chapter 1

AGNI - THE MESSENGER, THE PRIEST, THE ANGEL

(i) I glorify Agni, the divine priest and the messenger of my oblations to God who is the bestower of prosperity. (Ṛ. 1-1-1)

(ii) May Agni, the divine priest, who is glorified by both the past and the present sages, increase and strengthen our bond with the Dēvas. (Ṛ.1-1- 2)

(iii) Praying to God through Agni, the angel priest, may we, the worshippers, obtain valiant offspring and daily increasing prosperity and glory. (Ṛ. 1-1-3)

(iv) The divine Agni holds in His hands many good gifts for men. He conveys our prayers to the eternal Creator. The divine Agni bestows prosperity upon men. (Ṛ. 1-72-1)

(v) O Agni! Come and take your seat amidst us; hear our praises; and accept the oblations of foodgrains from us. Bless us with plenty of food. (Ṛ. 6-16-10)

Chapter 2

BLESSINGS

(a) Blessings to a Younger Person

(i) May you see all that needs to be seen;
May you listen to all that needs to be listened;
May you speak what needs to be spoken;
May your thinking be wholesome;
May you lead yourself to perfection. (Y. 6-15)

(ii) May you rise and not fall;
May you be granted long life;
May you achieve success in your occupation;
May you ride the chariot of happiness; and
May you grow in wisdom with years. (A. 8-1-6)

(iii) May the Earth and the Heaven be auspicious and troublefree for you.
May the sunshine bring you blessings;
May the wind bring you good luck; and
May the rivers bring you plenty of clear water for your good. (A. 8- 2-14)

(iv) May the wind purify you;
May the waters bring you immortality;
May the warmth of the sun bless your bodies;
May death spare you so that you may live long. (A. 8-1-5)

(b) God Bless the Prayerful

(i) May those who offer prayers to God not commit heinous sin.
May those who praise God not experience decay.
May God-loving people always be helped by other people.
May afflictions fall on only those who never offer prayers.
(Ṛ. 1- 125-7)

(ii) O God! We welcome your help for the destruction of our maladies. We invoke you to bless us with children and grandchildren. (Ṛ. 10-9-3)

(iii) God bestows prosperity on the person who worships. God blesses such a person. The worshipper is the one who can be called wise. (Y. 17- 52)

(iv) Lord! Be our preserver. Look after us and be merciful to us, your worshippers. You are the friend, the most loving father, giving to us land and food. (Ṛ. 4-17-17)

(v) Would I be able to establish communion with the Lord (Varuṇa)?
Would I be able to reach Him?
Would He accept my offerings with pleasure?
When with a happy heart will I be able to receive His mercy? (Ṛ. 7-86-2)

Chapter 3

BUSINESS

Prayer for Success in Business

O Lord! It has been a long and hard road.
Please accept our oblations and prayers for the success of our business.
May our purchases and sales be profitable.
May our transactions bring prosperity. (A. 3-15-4)

Chapter 4

CHARITY

(i) Wonderful rewards await those who give pious gifts. The sun shines in heaven for such persons. They enjoy a long happy life in this world and indeed attain immortality.
(Ṛ. 1-125-6)

(ii) Lord, Give power to his speech and grant him prosperity who serves you through his noble actions and charity.
(Ṛ. 6-16-26)

(iii) Charity to the needy is a good way of worshipping the Lord. It is a blessing and a privilege which is not available to non-believers and to those who indulge in sinful actions. Prayers and worship by sinners do not please God. Only those who stay away from sins and from denigrating others and make a pious gift to God are the ones who are able to please God. (Ṛ. 10-107-3)

(iv) God withholds his favors from the rich person who is Godless and who is not interested in giving charity.
(Ṛ. 1-150-2)

(v) The inhospitable person acquires wealth in vain. I tell you sincerely that he is working on his own downfall. He is in favor with neither God nor men. The rich person who does not share is a sinner. (Ṛ. 10-117-6)

(vi) (Remember you rich persons!)
The poor and the hungry are not the only ones who die. The rich and well-fed die too. The wealth of the rich man who generously gives, does not run out. On the other hand, the world has no sympathy for the rich person who does not give. (Ṛ. 10-117-1)

(vii) A wicked person who maligns others by his speech, thinks ill of others, refrains from charity, and indulges in deceit and trickery, hurts himself by his own such deeds. (Ṛ.1-147-4)

(viii) Glorious Lord! Instigate the niggard to become generous and charitable. Soften the heart of the miser. (Ṛ. 6-53-3)

(ix) O Lord! Because of your grace men live unharmed, are blessed with children, and become wealthy. May your generosity go to those who are generous in giving horses, cows, and clothing (to those in need). (Ṛ. 5-42-8)

Chapter 5

CONTENTMENT

Prayer Seeking Contentment

O Lord! Let contentment come to
my mind;
my speech;
my breath;
my eyes;
my ears;
my soul;
my progeny; and to
the people around me.
Let the people around me never suffer a longing of any kind.

(Y. 6-31)

Chapter 6

CREATION

(i) How did the earth and the sky come into being? In what order were the various components of the universe created?

No one knows; not even the most learned amongst us. All we know is that the day and night keep revolving as though mounted on a wheel. (Ṛ. 1-185-1)

(ii) Systematically, Lord, the creator, brought forth the sun, and the moon, the heaven, and the earth, the atmosphere, and the days and nights. (Ṛ. 10-190-3)

(iii) The all-knowing Lord created the earth and the sky using his divine powers. How he began and accomplished it, is a question which has not been answered yet. (Ṛ. 10-81-2)

(iv) Nāsadīya Hymn

In the beginning there was neither existence nor non-existence. There was neither air nor space. There was no water, deep and fathomless. There was nothing to envelope or protect. (Ṛ. 10-129-1)

There was neither death nor immortality. There was neither night nor day. Only God breathed windless by His own power. Apart from God there was nothing whatsoever. (Ṛ. 10-129-2)

Darkness was enveloped by darkness everywhere before the creation of the universe. Yet there subsisted one glorious Being, all intelligence, who created the universe by contemplation of what he wanted to do. (Ṛ. 10-129-3)

We men do not really know. Who can therefore tell, how this universe was created and when? Even the angels may have come into existence after the universe was created. No one can tell. (Ṛ. 10-129-6)

Some people ask : "Did the elemental matter, from which this Universe was built, always exist or was it also created by God?"

The One who built and controls this universe alone knows. If He does not know then who knows? (Ṛ. 10-129-7)

Chapter 7

DEATH

(a) Save Me from Death - Spare My Life The Mṛtyuñjaya Mantra

O Lord! The fragrance of Your glory is a source of strength to me. My breath is attached to my body just like a cucumber is attached to the cucumber plant. I pray to you - do not separate my breath from my body. Protect me from death. Grant me immortality.

(Ṛ. 7-59-12)

Commentary

This mantra is repeatedly chanted on behalf of the person who is so sick that he may die. God is prayed with this mantra for sparing the life of this person.

(b) To the Spirit of the Dead

O Spirit of the dead! Go to the highest heaven and meet with Yama and your ancestors. Carry with you only the good karma leaving behind the bad. Seek a body and a new home, and a life of glory. (Ṛ. 10- 14-8)

Chapter 8

DEVOTION

Prayers of Devotion

(i) O Lord, the remover of darkness! We pray to you every morning and evening with sincere thoughts of reverence. Through our prayer we come close to you. (Ṛ. 1-1-7)

(ii) O Lord! We recognize you amidst the enlightened persons. They are the closest to you. We implore you not to pass us by. We ask you to come to us and give us enlightenment. (Ṛ. 1-4-3)

(iii) Lord! How do I comprehend you?
Let my ears be turned to hear you;
Let my eyes be opened to behold you;
Let my mind be eager to know you;
Let my heart be absorbed in you.
What more shall I say? (Ṛ. 6-9-6)

(iv) Come ye all, with your full grace, to the glorious Lord! He is the One to whom all pathways turn. He indeed is the One. (S. 372)

(v) O God! O Gaṇapati!
Among us, your subjects, You are our master. Hail to you.
Among those who are wise, You are the wisest.
Among superiors, You are the highest lord.
Among the glorious, You are the most glorious.
Among the souls, You are the Supreme Soul.
With this prayer, lord, we are asking You to bless us with your presence in our midst to give us Your protection.
(Ṛ. 2-23-1)

(vi) O God! O Gaṇapati!
Among us your subjects, you are our master. Hail to you.
Among the beloved, you are the most beloved. Hail to you.
Among assets, you are the greatest asset. Hail to you.
You live within us and know us from the time we come in the womb.
Yes, since we come in the womb. (Y. 23-19)

Commentary

In the above two prayers God is addressed as Gaṇapati. During Vedic times Gaṇapati was an epithet of Dēva Bṛhaspati. Later Gaṇapati or Gaṇēśa was given a form and parents.

Chapter 9

DHARMA

Dharma Upholds the Earth

The qualities of truthfulness, righteousness, daring, and hard work, combined with belief in God, prayer, and charity, are what upholds a nation.

May our country, the mistress of our past, present, and future, open wide opportunities for us. (A. 12-1-1)

Commentary

The first paragraph above describes the constituents of Dharma.

Chapter 10

DIVINITY IN MAN

Wise people know that human body is a temple of God. All the Dēvas live inside the human body just as cows live in the cowshed.
(A. 11-8-32)

O men! You do not know the Supreme Lord who has created all the stars and the planets, and all the living beings. You, yourself, have within you the divine element.

Ignorant persons remain satisfied with acquiring their physical needs and with chanting the mantras without understanding what they represent. These men are unable to reach the divine within.
(Ṛ. 10- 82-7)

Commentary

This Ṛgvedic hymn is extremely important, in that it, perhaps, was the inspiration for the philosophy of the Upaniṣads. In the Upaniṣads, the divine element mentioned in this hymn was expounded as the individual soul and as part of the Supreme Soul. Also this mantra stresses the need for acquiring wisdom which is the central theme of the Upaniṣads. It is remarkable that countless Hindūs and persons of other faiths read or chant parts of their scriptures without understanding their meaning. Many Hindūs even chant verses and so-called mantras which are not true scriptures and have undesirable meanings and consequences, simply because they have not cared to know the meaning of what they are chanting.

Chapter 11

FAITH IN GOD

(i) Viewing both truth and falsehood, God classified the lack of faith in Him to falsehood and faith in Him to truth.

(Y. 19-77)

(ii) By holy resolve does one obtain consecration.
By consecration does one gain grace.
By grace does one develop trust in God.
Trust in God leads one to the Truth. (Y. 19-30)

Chapter 12

FEARLESSNESS

The following prayers and statements show that fearlessness is a very important ingredient of the Hindū dharma. Hindū scriptures ask Hindūs not to be afraid of anyone or anything except the displeasure of God arising out of sinful deeds.

(i) May the Heaven and the Earth Grant us fearlessness.
May the boundless space breathe fearlessness in us.
May the Saptarṣi (seven stars of the Great Bear) breathe fearlessness in us. (A. 6-40-1)

(ii) May the skies make us fearless;
May the earth make us fearless;
May the heaven make us fearless;
May fearlessness envelope us from the front, from behind, from below, and from up above. (A. 19-15-5)

(iii) May I be fearless of the friend, fearless of the foe, fearless of the known, and fearless of the unknown.
May my days be without fear and my nights without fear.
Let the whole world desire to be friendly with me.
(A. 19-15-6)

(iv) In this wide world O Lord, we need your continuous guidance. You are the heavenly beacon of light with infinite wisdom. Bless us to becoming fearless and highly motivated. We surrender ourselves O Lord, into your strong arms. (Ṛ. 6-47-8)

(v) God! Make us fearless by guarding us against whatever troubles could come to us. Give your blessings to our children and security to our animals. (Y. 36-22)

Chapter 13

FORGIVENESS

Prayers Seeking Forgiveness

(i) My conduct may have been, at times, uncooperative and unjustifiably rebellious. I may not have spoken the complete truth at times; and I may have used harsh language. I know that all this behavior is sinful. God! Let this water wash away from me this sinful behavior. (Ṛ. 1-23-22)

(ii) God! If through ignorance, through unmindfulness, through conceit, or through human weaknesses we have committed offense against you or against men, we pray to you to pardon us. (Ṛ. 4-54-3)

(iii) If we have done wrong to the earth, the space, or the heavens; or, if we have offended our mother or father, may the good Lord forgive us and guide us to perform good deeds. (A. 6-120-1)

Chapter 14

FRIENDLINESS

Prayer and Statement

(i) Lord! Make me strong.
May all look on me with the eye of a friend;
May I look on all with the eye of a friend;
May we all be cordial to each other. (Y. 36-18)

(ii) I look at people with friendliness, and
I talk to them cordially. They do the same to me.
Yet, I am strong and energetic enough to thwart the attempts of those who are unfriendly and who want to hurt me. (A. 12-1-58)

(iii) Let us be helpful to others.
Let us lend as much assistance to others as possible.
Let us be cordial to others. (Ṛ. 10-97-14)

(iv) May the Earth that bears people speaking varied languages, with various religious rites according to places of abode, enrich me with wealth in a thousand streams, like a milch cow that never fails. (A. 12-1-45)

Commentary

The verse acknowledges that the earth belongs to different races, speaking different languages and following different religions. This is a commitment for mutual respect.

Chapter 15

GAMBLING

(i) My wife is good natured. She never quarrelled with me. She was loving to me and kind to my friends. I have driven her away from me because of my addiction to gambling. (Ṛ. 10-34-2)

(ii) My wife has rejected me; and my mother-in-law dislikes me. No one is offering to help me – a compulsive gambler, who has lost everything. I am as unwanted as an old horse. (Ṛ. 10-34-3)

(iii) Do not play with dice. Till your land and rejoice in your income and property so obtained, feeling great about it. Consider yourself fortunate for possessing your cattle and having your wife with you. This is the message that Lord Savitar has revealed to me. (Ṛ. 10-34-13)

Chapter 16

GĀYATRĪ MANTRA

The prayer Seeking Wisdom

(The Earth, the Sky, and the Heaven praise Him.) Let us meditate on the glory of the divine Lord. He is the One who sustains us. We pray to Him that He may direct our understanding by instilling wisdom in us. (Ṛ. 3-62-10)

Commentary

This is the most famous of all Vedic mantras, and is called Gāyatrī mantra after the meter in which it is composed. "Ōṃ Bhūr, bhuvaḥ, svaḥ" are not part of the mantra. Ōṃ is always put at the beginning of a mantra, or a set of mantras. "bhūr, bhuvaḥ, svaḥ" the set of three words, is called vyāhṛti. It is always prefixed to this mantra and also to many other mantras.

Chapter 17

GOD

(a) There is only one God

(i) There are no eight, nine, or ten Gods;
There are no five, six, or seven Gods;
There are not even two, three, or four Gods;
To him who knows, there is only one God.
All deities are but different names of the One.
He is the One, the only One.
He is the One who oversees what breathes and what does not breathe.
He is the One with all the power and the authority.
(A. 13-4-15/21)

(ii) The wise seers in their adoration make into many forms the One Supreme. (Ṛ. 10-114-5)

(iii) God is almighty. He is the One and only. In Him all the dēvas become unified. (A. 13-4-12/13)

(iv) The wise sages know; and they tell us about the One unborn Lord who upholds the universe. (Ṛ. 1-164-6)

(v) There is that One God they call by so many names: Indra, Mitra, Varuṇa, Agni, Garutmat, Yama, Mātariśvan.
(Ṛ. 1-164-46)

(vi) Many people ask who God is. He is our parent and ruler. He is our preserver. He knows everything and everyone. All the deities are Him, the One and only. Yet, human beings keep asking who he is. (Ṛ. 10-82-3)

(vii) (The heaven holds in its bosom the planets, the stars, the sun, and the moon, just as the earth holds the living beings and non-living things.) The heaven and the earth grant to every one born a distinct identity; yet all life, moving and stationery, depends on one Supreme Being. (Ṛ. 3-54-8)

(viii) The sage beholds the Being who dwells in us all and pervades the entire universe. In that Being is the union of all there is. This Being is the warp and woof of all creatures. (Y. 32-8)

(ix) One is Agni (fire) kindled in various ways;
One is Sūrya (sun) shining over all;
One is Uṣas (dawn) illuminating all things;
That one has become this all. (Ṛ. 8-58-2)

(b) God is Omnipresent

(i) Whether two men are sitting down or moving, doing things in secret, or whispering, they should remember that there is always that third One present - the omnipresent ruler of the world. (A. 4-16-2)

(ii) The empire of the king of the earth and the boundless skies, is far-flung. The two mighty oceans are his loins and yet He resides in a tiny drop of water. (A. 4-16-3)

(iii) The Supreme Lord has his eyes in every direction. His hands stretch out to reach every place. With His feet He instantaneously reaches everywhere. He is the one who has created this whole universe. He is the One and only, who rewards and punishes. (Ṛ. 10-81-3)

(iv) The most glorious Lord is in the clouds, the sky, the heaven, and everywhere else. Recognize him in the guest visiting with you. He is present in all men and in greater measure in the body of the priest and virtuous men. He is reachable through worship and through the path of truth and virtue. (Ṛ. 4-40-5)

(c) God is Generous

(i) Our Earth!
This our earth is immense;
It provides us abundance;
It is all sustaining — all nourishing;
It has room for entire mankind whom it so graciously supports;
We can see clearly that our earth is not hostile to us.
(Y. 13-18)

(ii) God created this earth to give it to mankind for a home. The generous Lord has created a big wide world for the human race. (Ṛ. 7-100-4)

(iii) O Earth!
You are the stable support of all beings.
You preserve our lives.

You grant us vigor; and
You provide us a place to abide, and
to cultivate our crops. (Y. 14-21)

(iv) On this majestic earth with hills and snow-capped mountains, with forests and rivers running blue waters, with black, brown, and red soils that sustain us, do I walk under the protection of the Lord, unslain, unwounded, undefeated. (A. 12-1-11)

(v) Lord! No one can point to the limits of your glorious deeds! No one can assert that you are not generous in giving. (Ṛ. 8-32-15)

(vi) O God! You give us the love of a loving father; the help of one who cares; and the friendship of a true friend. (Ṛ. 1-26-3)

(d) The Laws of God

God's laws are excellent and eternal. No one can break or disobey them – neither the conniving enemies of men nor the wisest among us. Not even the earth or the heaven can challenge them. They are like mountains which never bend. (Ṛ. 3-56-1)

(e) The Will of God

Whatever God desires, that assuredly comes to pass. No man can change God's will. (Ṛ. 8-28-4)

(f) Finding God

(i) God is divine, yet He is also human.
God is, from whom everything emerges, and
God is, to whom everything goes back.
God is, our friend and yet, men do not know Him.
(A. 4-16-8)

(ii) Lord!
You are (in) the man;
You are (in) the woman;
You are (in) the child;
You are (in) the old person;
You exist in all of us, and you exist everywhere.
(A. 10-8-27)

(g) The Glory of God

Prayers

(i) What God shall we worship with our oblations?
The One who existed in the beginning and who is the prime cause of the elements; the One who upholds the Earth and the Sky; the One who is the lord of all living beings.
(Ṛ. 10-121-1)

(ii) What God shall we worship with our oblations?
The One who is the bestower of life and vigor;
The One whose commandments the cosmic forces carry out;
The One who bestows immortality or death. (Ṛ. 10-121-2)

(iii) What God shall we worship with our oblations?
The One who, by his power and greatness, rules eternally over men and animals, all of whom assume life for a fleeting moment. (Ṛ. 10-121-3)

(iv) What God shall we worship with our oblations?
The One who made the solid earth and the vast sky;
The One who runs the solar system and makes water go up to become rain clouds. (Ṛ. 10-121-5)

(v) God! You deserve all the glory.
May we gain your full attention through loving prayers.
May those who sing your praises receive your love.
(Ṛ. 1-10-12)

(vi) In His stride the Lord (Viṣṇu) took three steps and the whole universe was collected in the dust of His feet. Hail to the Lord! (Ṛ. 1-22-17)

(vii) O Lord Viṣṇu! The wise know that you are the omnipresent supreme. You extend over and beyond the range of sky as the eye that can see everything. (Ṛ. 1-22-20)

(viii) O Almighty Lord!
Your power and reach are praiseworthy. No one dare harm your devotees. (Ṛ. 1-27-8)

(ix) God!
You clothe the naked;
You heal the sick;
You can make the blind see; and
You can make the cripple walk. (Ṛ. 8-79-2)

(x) I trust you Lord! to be holier than the holiest;
I trust you Lord! to be the mover of the immovable;
I trust you Lord! to be stronger than the strongest;
I trust you Lord! to be wiser than the wisest. (Ṛ. 8-96-4)

(xi) Salutations to you O God!
- the granter of welfare;
- the source of happiness;
- the beneficent;
- the cause of joy;
- the auspicious;
- the source of greatest bliss. (Y. 16-41)

(xii) God is the fire. He is the waters. He is the wind; and He is the sun and moon. He is the splendor; and He is the lord of all there is. (Y. 32-1)

(xiii) The Lord is our creator!
He is the cause of everything.
He is our friend.
We know that the whole universe is his abode; and He is imperishable.
Be meditating upon Him we obtain immortality. (Y. 32-10)

(xiv) We pay our homage to Him and Him only — the glorious Lord to whom the entire past belonged and to whom belongs the entire future. (A. 10-8-1)

(xv) Let us pay our homage in the morning, during the day, in the evening, and during the night, to the Lord who grants us life and who also takes it away. (A. 11-2-16)

(xvi) Would someone teach me about the One Lord in whom the earth, the skies, and the heaven subsist; and who is the support of the sun, the moon, the fire, and the wind?

(A. 10-7-12)

(xvii) He, without whose blessing men do not conquer the enemy; whom when going to the battlefield we invoke; whose divine power the universe reflects; He O men, is the Lord.

(Ṛ. 2-12-9)

Chapter 18

Good Deeds

(i) Let the words of truth be spoken.
Let the deeds of wisdom be performed. (Ṛ. 1-123-6)

(ii) May I travel the Lord's favorite path, which is the delight of God-seeking men; and which leads me to wide-stepping Viṣṇu, the friend of the pious, and whose abode is all bliss. (Ṛ. 1-154-5)

Chapter 19

GOOD LIFE

Prayers Seeking Good Life and Happiness

(i) O Lord! Hear my prayer and invocation. Make this day a happy one. Protect me today. (Ṛ. 1-25-19)

(ii) O the Earth! Make yourself a pleasant place for us to settle down. Let our life on earth be troublefree. Let there be no wickedness and injury in our life on this planet. (Y. 35-21)

(iii) Lord! Help us attain our objectives. Help us acquire a sharp mind. Grant us food. Make us prosperous. (Ṛ. 1-5-3)

(iv) God! You are the mightiest. You can make us mortals happy. There is no one who can comfort men except you. We pray to you with these words of praise. (Ṛ. 1-84-19)

(v) God! May we listen with our ears to what is good;
May we see with our eyes what is good;
May we with firm limbs enjoy the term of life granted to us, singing your praises. (Ṛ. 1-89-8)

(vi) Aditi! I pray to you for prosperity; for a life without injury and pain. I pray for abundance of food.
Protect us from all kinds of dangers and evil forces.
(Ṛ. 1-185-3)

(vii) Lord, make me immortal in a world in which my desires are fulfilled and where happiness and joy dwell. (Ṛ. 9-113-11)

(viii) O Lord! Grant us prosperity;
Grant us the gift of an undecaying body;
Grant us physical strength and purity of mind;
Grant us a life of glory. (Y. 2-24)

(ix) O Lord ! I pray to you to grant me long life, intelligence, good offspring, and prosperity. (Y. 3-19)

(x) May my prayers be answered,
and may I be granted
- strength;
- creativity;
- endeavor;
- honesty;
- understanding;
- determination;
- strong voice;
- glory;
- patience to listen;
- ability to communicate;
- ability to observe; and lastly
- a place in heaven.
May God make all these wishes come true. (Y. 18-1)

(xi) May my prayers be answered,
and May I be granted
- my welfare and of those I hold dear;
- cheerfulness;

- love;
- grace;
- excellence;
- prosperity; and
- glory.

May God make all these wishes come true. (Y. 18-8)

Chapter 20

HEALTH AND LONG LIFE

Prayers Seeking Health and Long Life

(i) O God!
Bestow on us bounteous wealth;
Bless us with good minds;
Give us healthy bodies, sweet speech, and fair days.
(Ṛ. 2-21-6)

(ii) God! You have ordained hundred years as the life of man; please do not cut our life shorter.
Pray do not make us so infirm in our last years that we may need the paternal care of our children. (Ṛ. 1-89-9)

(iii) May waters be available for our crops. May waters be available for growing medicinal herbs which will keep us away from disease and afford us long life. (Ṛ. 10-9-7)

(iv) O God! You have blessed us with so many medicinal plants. With the help of the cures you have provided, may I sustain myself well so that I could keep busy in productive work for a life-span of hundred years. Not only may I keep sickness out of my body, I should also remove sinful thoughts from my mind, and, in particular, ill-will against any fellow man.
(Ṛ. 2-33-2)

(v) God! May we see 'the bright eye' (the sunrise) for a hundred years. May we be granted

a hundred years to live;
a hundred years to see well;
a hundred years to hear well;
a hundred years to speak clearly;
a hundred years of self-dependence;
Yes, all of the above; and even in excess of hundred years.
(Y. 36- 24)

(vi) May I live a hundred summers;
May I retain my eyesight a hundred summers;
May I retain my mental faculty a hundred summers;
May my wisdom continue to grow a hundred summers;
May I retain my strength a hundred summers;
May I remain pure and sinless a hundred summers;
Yes, May I achieve all of the above for even more than a hundred summers. (A. 19-67-1/8)

(vii) O Lord! So long as I breathe
May my voice remain clear;
May my sight remain unimpaired;
May my hearing remain intact;
May my hair not turn gray;
May my teeth remain white;
May my arms remain strong;
May my thighs remain powerful;
May my legs remain strong;
May my feet remain stable;
May all of my limbs remain intact;
May my soul ever remain untainted. (A. 19-60-2)

Chapter 21

HOME

(a) Prayer at the Site of the New Home

Right here do I erect a firm house.
May it stand on a strong foundation, dripping with prosperity.
May our family, which will live here, consist of brave people.
(A. 3- 12-1)

(b) Prayers at Gṛhapraveśa (House-warming)

(i) We bring to this house water which is free from disease and which is curative.
We bring to this house fire immortal;
With these we set our feet in this house and take possession of it. (A. 3-12-9)

(ii) O Lord of this dwelling!
Recognize us. Let this house bring us comfort. Protect us from ill-health. Be pleased to fulfill our dreams. Bestow your blessings upon us and on our animals. (Ṛ. 7-54-1)

(iii) O Lord of this dwelling!
Be our protector and preserver. Augment our wealth. May we, through your friendship, become exempt from decay. Be caring to us like a father is to his children. (Ṛ. 7-54-2)

(iv) O Lord of this dwelling!
May we be possessed of a comfortable, delightful, opulent abode, granted by you. Protect our wealth whether in our possession or yet to come. Cherish us forever with your blessings. (Ṛ. 7-54-3)

(v) From the eastern direction,
From the southern direction.
From the western direction.
From the northern direction.
From the depths below.
From the heights above;
I summon a blessing, to the glory of this house.
Praise be to God, the praiseworthy, forever and ever.
(A. 9-3-25/31)

(c) Prayer by Visitors to a Home

O Lord! Let this home be one in which love abounds, such that a person visiting this home always remembers it.
Let us be welcome in this home. (Y. 3-42)

Chapter 22

LOVE & UNITY

(a) The Power of Love

You, O Love, are greater than all.
You are higher than heaven, and wider than earth.
You, O Love, are greater than all.
You are swifter than wind, and hotter than fire.
You, O Love, are greater than all. (A. 9-2-20 and 24)

(b) Love and Unity

(i) God said, "I want you to be of one heart and one mind, devoid of hate.
Love one another as the cow loves her newborn calf."
(A. 3-30-1)

(ii) Let the son be devoted to his father;
Let him be of one mind with his mother;
Let the wife be sweet and gentle to her husband.
(A. 3-30-2)

(iii) Let brother not hate brother;
Let sister not hate sister;
Let the family-members be united in heart, be of one goal, and speak sweetly with each other. (A. 3-30-3)

(iv) In working with others, may we follow the example of our elders, and work in cooperation and with discipline.
May we be united in resolve, and pleasant in communication.
(A. 3-30-5)

(v) Congregate. Speak with one another. Bring your minds into accord. Pray together as our sages in the past always did.
(Ṛ. 10-191-2)

(vi) May we assemble, for the worship of the Lord, to pray together, like spokes around the hub of a wheel.
May we eat and drink together. (A. 3-30-6)

(vii) The Lord Spoke - "I render you of common goal, and of united mind. Follow your chosen leader. Let the immortal Dēvas protect you and may you be happy night and day."
(A. 3-30-7)

(viii) May our assembly be common;
May our minds be common;
May our prayers be common, and
May our purpose be common.
With these wishes we offer Thee our oblations.
(Ṛ. 10-191-3)

(ix) United be our resolves;
United be our hearts;
United be our spirits;
May we live together (in a nation) in unity and brotherhood.
(R. 10-191-4)

(c) Unity Necessary for Defense

Worship does not go in vain.

God is our protector. He wants us to enjoy our life. When danger faces us from outside he wants us to face it by uniting together and by so doing obtain victory. (Ṛ. 1-179-3)

God is our lord and master. He is our parent and well-wisher. He is our support. He wants us to acquire wisdom and unity among ourselves. Unanimity of thought and action in our society will make us strong. (A. 7-20-1)

Chapter 23

MṚTYUÑJAYA MANTRA

Prayer for Sparing Life

O Lord! The fragrance of Your glory is a source of strength to me. My breath is attached to my body just like a cucumber is attached to the cucumber plant. I pray to you — do not separate my breath from my body. Protect me from death. Grant me immortality.

(Ṛ. 7-59-12)

Commentary

In the times of Ṛgvēda the word tryambaka, perhaps, referred to three Goddesses - Bhāratī, Iḷā, and Sarasvatī, being called the three mothers. Later on Trayambaka began to be used for Śiva, the three-eyed lord. The words "urvārukam iva bandhanān mṛtyor mukṣīya" have been translated by some as - "as cucumbers separate from its plant so God you separate us from death". This translation, though literal, does not seem proper because cucumbers separate from the cucumber plant when they ripen and so should the breath separate from the body only when the body gets old. It is, therefore, better to interpret these words as though the prayer is asking God not to separate the breath from the body.

Chapter 24

PEACE INVOCATION

Let us be in peace and harmony with our earth and with the skies.
Let us be in harmony with the waters and with the plant kingdom;
Let us be in harmony with the forests.
Let us be in peace and harmony with the Dēvas.
May we dedicate this invocation for harmony everywhere.
May the Lord make a gift of peace to us and to all men.
May harmony be established by removing what is dreadful.
May harmony be established by removing what is sinful.
May peace and harmony reign everywhere. (A. 19-9-14)

May we be in peace and harmony with the heaven, the sky, and the earth.
May we be in harmony with the waters.
May we be in harmony with the plant-kingdom.
May we be in harmony with all the Dēvas (divine powers), and, therefore, with God.
May peace and harmony reign everywhere.

(Y. 36-14)

Chapter 25

PRAYERS ASKING GOD FOR FAVORS

(a) Protect Us

(i) May Dēvas be beneficent to us. May Dēvas, our sustainers, be beneficent to us. May Dēvas be beneficent to us willingly and generously. May Heaven and Earth be beneficient to us. May our prayers bring us beneficent response. (Ṛ. 7-35-3)

(ii) God! Make us walk erect. Protect us by your splendor, from evil. Vanquish the evil. Allow us to make our journey through life saying our prayers to you. (Ṛ. 1-36-14)

(iii) May auspicious powers exercise judgment in our favor. May the powers allowing us unobstructed pure life burst through in our favor. May the Dēvas always augment our family-welfare indeed. May the Almighty protect us day after day. (Ṛ. 1-89-1)

(iv) O Dēvas! Shower your benevolence upon us. May you be generous to us ever, approving of the righteous among us. May we obtain your friendship; and may you grant us long life. (Ṛ. 1-89-2)

(v) Lord!
Protect us from the west;
Protect us from the east;
Protect us from the north;

Protect us from the south;
Grant us prosperity; and
Grant us long life. (Ṛ. 10-36-14)

(vi) O Lord! You are the protector.
We bring our adoration and reverence to you.
Guard our lives and those of our children.
Protect our animals. (A. 3-15-7)

(vii) O God! The giver of life to us all! You are my master!
When I am praying;
When I am discharging my duties;
When I am performing my priestly functions;
When I am deep in thought;
When I am in the process of defining my purposes;
When I am in the company of learned people;
in all these situations please protect me (by showing me the right direction. (A. 5-24-1)

(viii) O God ! O Gaṇapati!
Among us, your subjects, You are our master. Hail to you.
Among those who are wise, You are the wisest.
Among superiors, You are the highest lord.
Among the glorious, You are the most glorious.
Among the souls, You are the Supreme Soul.
With this prayer, Lord, we are asking You to bless us with your presence in our midst to give us Your protection. (R. 2-23-1)

(b) Give Us Children

(i) The most respectable, the imperishable, and the most righteous Dēvas were prayed by Manu, the progenitor. Today we pray to them to bless us with a child who will grow up and attain glory. May we be blessed by you O Lord. (Ṛ. 7-35-15)

(ii) May the prayerful couples be blessed with sons and daughters; and may such couples enjoy their full span of life in prosperity, decked with gold. (Ṛ. 8-31-8)

(iii) I am a mortal and you are eternal, O God! I praise you with devotion; and ask you of two favors. That we may earn glory, and that we may gain immortality through an unbroken line of descendants. (Ṛ. 5-4-10)

(c) Give Us Prosperity and Happiness

(i) Lord! We bring to You our adoration!
Lead us through the righteous path to riches.
Lord! You know every sacred duty.
Remove the thoughts from our minds that make us stray and wander. (Ṛ. 1-189-1)

(ii) I am desirous of prosperity for the sake of making generous gifts. May heaven and earth attend me with favor. (Ṛ. 1-185-9)

(iii) God! Be unto us easy of access, as is a father to his son. Be ever present in our midst, giving us happiness. (Ṛ. 1-1-9)

(d) Give Us Healthy Water

(i) The clean, healthy, and tasteful water is as beneficial as a mother's milk is to the infant. May this water keep nourishing us. (Ṛ. 10-9-2)

(d) Give Us Glory

(i) I am a mortal and your are eternal, O God! I praise you with devotion and ask you two favors: That we may earn glory, and that we may gain immortality through an unbroken line of descendants. (Ṛ. 5-4-10)

(ii) O Lord!
May I receive glory on the earth and in heaven. May Indra, Bṛhaspati, and Bhaga be on my side. May I be blessed with prosperity, and devotion to you. May I carry your message forcefully to fellow human beings. May I, along with this entire congregation, be blessed with everlasting glory.
(S. 611)

Chapter 26

RULER OF THE COUNTRY

A Prayer for the Ruler

O Bṛhaspati and Savitar! Make our king knowledgeable. Even though he is bright, make his intellect sharper. Exalt him to great heights. Let all the Dēvas be pleased with him. (Y. 27-8)

Chapter 27

ŚAṂ NŌ DĒVĪ MANTRA

Gratitude for Drinking Water

May the divine waters be propitious to us. May the streams of good drinking water be flowing to us for our preservation and health. (Ṛ. 10-9-4)

Chapter 28

SERVICE OF HUMANITY

(i) O Divine Agni! Your generosity is like that of the stream of water that flows down the mountain slopes to provide comfort to the parched earth. We ask you to instill in us the same magnanimity as you have, so that we get busy benefitting others. (Ṛ. 3-57-6)

(ii) O Agni! The seated Yajamāna (host) is sharing the worship with us (while bearing the entire cost of the worship ceremony).
His family has set a superior example, among us, of personal piety and actions in the service of others.
We ask the Dēvas to wake all of us up to our sense of piety and service of others. (Y. 15-54)

Chapter 29

SIN, REPENTANCE, AND PURIFICATION

(i) O most gracious Lord! You bring the world to life and you maintain its stability. You control the animate and the inanimate. Grant us freedom from three types of sin — sins of improper thinking, improper speech, and improper action. (Ṛ. 4-53-6)

(ii) Lord! I am not in control of myself and that is the reason I have been a sinner. Alcohol, anger, gambling, and ignorance have led me into the wrong path. Even in dreams am I not free of sin. (Ṛ. 7-86-6)

(iii) O Dēvas! Please purify me, cleanse my heart and my mind. Cleanse my whole being. Cleanse the hearts of mankind. (Y. 19-39)

(iv) Lord! You see it all because you are present everywhere. You notice our sins. May we be repentant of our sins. (Ṛ. 1-97-6)

(v) We may have committed sins against friends and family members. We repentantly pray to you for forgiveness, because these are sins against You, O Dēvas. (Ṛ. 1-185-8)

(vi) O God! Forgive if I have ever committed sin against a benefactor, a dear friend, a companion, my brother, my neighbor, or a stranger. (Ṛ. 5-85-7)

(vii) O God! We may have committed the sin of blaming others in error just like gamblers do when they argue; we may have knowingly committed sin; or we may have unknowingly performed evil deeds. We pray to you to rid us of all three kinds of sin so that we remain your beloved. (Ṛ. 5-85-8)

(viii) May we not commit sin against the Lord who has compassion even for those who commit sin. (Ṛ. 7-87-7)

(ix) O Protector Dēvas! Let not slumber or idle talk, critical of others, overtake us. (Ṛ. 8-48-14)

(x) May the omniscient Lord who rules over the animate and the inanimate, deliver us today from our sins of the past and of future, for our own good. (Ṛ. 10-63-8)

(xi) My conduct may have been, at times, uncooperative and unjustifiably rebellious. I may not have spoken the complete truth at times; and I may have used harsh language. I know that all this behavior is sinful. God! Let this water wash away from me this sinful behavior. (Ṛ. 1-23-22)

(xii) Charity to the needy is a good way of worshipping the Lord. It is a blessing and a privilege which is not available to the non-believers and those who indulge in sinful actions. Prayers and worship by sinners do not please God. Only those who stay away from sins and from denigrating others and make a pious gift to God are the ones who are able to please God. (Ṛ. 10-107-3)

(xiii) May Varuṇa, inspiring righteousness in us;
May Mitra, our friend and protector;
May Aryaman, calling us to remain active;
help us achieve our desires through straight (sinless) path,
and make our daily work joyful. (Ṛ. 1-90-1)

(xiv) May my priest offer my oblations to God. May the purpose of my mind be sincere. May I not fall into any kind of sin. May I be blessed by Dēvas. (Ṛ. 10-128-4)

(xv) Whatever sins we have committed in speaking to others, and in speaking of others, on purpose or inadvertently, in dream or when wide awake, O Lord! please remove far away from us such unworthy acts in future. (Ṛ. 10-164-3)

(xvi) Protect us God from the sin of slandering others. Pleased with our dedication (to virtue), become our friend. (Ṛ. 1-91-15)

Chapter 30

SOCIAL WISDOM - WORKING TOGETHER IN HARMONY

(i) In working with others, may we follow the example of our elders, and work in cooperation and with discipline.
May we be united in resolve, and pleasant in communication.
(A. 3-30- 5)

(ii) The Lord Spoke: "I render you of common goal, and of united mind. Follow your chosen leader. Let the immortal Dēvas protect you, and may you be happy night and day."
(A. 3-30-7)

(iii) May our assembly be common;
May our minds be common;
May our prayers be common, and
May our purpose be common.
With these wishes we offer Thee our oblations.
(Ṛ. 10-191-3)

(iv) Let the three Goddesses - Bhāratī, the Goddess of prosperity, Iḷā, the Goddess of power, and Sarasvatī, the Goddess of wisdom, come and sit down amidst us.
(Ṛ. 3-4-8)

Chapter 31

SPEECH

(i) With the first power of speech that you granted us, we gave names to things, O Lord!
You lovingly gave us the power to speak what is noble, and what without speech would be hidden in secrecy.
(Ṛ. 10-71-1)

(ii) God has created me from all of the 21 basic items of the universe. May he grant me the gift of eloquence. (A. 1-1-1)

(iii) In the company of learned people, the one who uses his faculty of speech meaningfully, courteously, and discretely, is called an able person. On the contrary, the person who opens his mouth fruitlessly, creating a lot of heat but no light, is like a cow that does not yield any milk, or like a tree that does not bear flowers and fruit. (Ṛ. 10-71-5)

(iv) If all speech could be divided into four equal parts, the wise will replace three parts with silence. (Ṛ. 1-164-45)

(v) Farmers use a sieve to separate out grain from chaff. Wise men use discretion as the sieve to speak only what should be spoken. The inner grace of a person shows up through the words spoken by him. It is through speech that great friendships are founded. (Ṛ. 10-71-2)

(vi) A wicked person who maligns others by his speech, thinks ill of others, refrains from charity, and indulges in deceit and trickery, hurts himself by his own such deeds. (Ṛ. 1-147-4)

(vii) O God! May I never bad-mouth the persons who are rich but charitable, who perform virtuous deeds, and those who are elders and worthy of respect. May wealth not make me arrogant; may you grant me virtuous children; and may I never fail to be worshipful to you. (Ṛ. 2-27-17)

(viii) O Protector Dēvas! Let not slumber or idle talk, critical of others, overtake us. (Ṛ. 8-48-14)

(ix) Protect us God from the sin of slandering others. Pleased with our dedication to virtue, be our friend. (Ṛ. 1-91-15)

(x) Sweet as honey may I begin;
Sweet as honey may I close; and
Sweet as honey may be my entire speech.
May my total being be sweet as honey. (A. 1-34-3)

(xi) Auspicious Aśvins! The true reality!
May my speech be as sweet as honey, so that I may convey your glorious message to mankind in a pleasing manner.
(A. 6-69-2)

Chapter 32

ŚRĪ RĀMA

I say my prayer in the presence of Duḥśīma, Pṛthu, Vēna, and the mighty king Rāma to whose chariot are yoked five hundred horses and whose renown is spread in all directions. (Ṛ. 10-93-14)

Chapter 33

STRENGTH AND VICTORY

Prayers Asking for Strength, Courage, and Victory

(i) O Lord! Grant us ever conquering might.
In each battle (whether against external foes, or internal foes such as lust, anger, etc.) give us manly strength. (S. 231)

(ii) God!
You are the fountain of glory! Grant me glory.
You are the fountain of courage! Grant me courage.
You are the fountain of power! Grant me strength.
You are the fountain of vigor! Grant me vigor;
You are the fountain of zeal! Grant me zeal. (Y. 19-9)

God!
May we conquer poverty by removing ignorance.
May we conquer hunger by being productive.
May we conquer battles by being valiant. (R. 10-43-10)

Commentary

The Hindūs of the Vedic period were kind to good people but were valiant fighters against those who wanted to hurt them. They prayed to God to give them unity, might, and courage to defend themselves against the enemy and be victorious in battle.

Chapter 34

SUICIDE AND KILLING OF CONSCIENCE

To the worlds which are sunless or demoniac, and which are covered with blinding gloom, go, after death, those persons who (commit suicide or who) kill their conscience. (Y. 40-3)

Commentary

Conscience is that part of a human being which relates him to his soul. Killing of conscience is equal to rendering your own soul ineffective. Since human soul is the God within, it means that a person though living has virtually killed himself spiritually. A different interpretation points out to the committing of suicide.

Chapter 35

THANKFULNESS

(i) Lord – the excellent and the beneficent!
We invoke you and thank you for the gifts which you have so graciously apportioned to us. You certainly watch over us.
(Ṛ. 1-22-7)

(ii) O Loving God!
This whole world with its wealth belongs to you. You are the One who has given us life. You give us the love and protection of a father. You are our friend. You make us strong and brave. You defend the doers of virtuous deeds. You make it possible for men to acquire hundreds and thousands of material possessions.
Good men flock to you. (Ṛ. 1-31-10)

(iii) O Lord! Because of your grace men live unharmed, are blessed with children, and become wealthy. May your generosity go to those who are generous in giving horses, cows, and clothing (to those in need). (Ṛ. 5-42-8)

Chapter 36

VIRTUE

(i) The ṛcās of the Ṛgvēda Saṃhitā and the Sāmas of the Sāmavēda Saṃhitā are prayer mantras of the scripture. They benefit the one who is awake (to his duties). To him God whispers, "I am yours, and I will remain your friend".
(Ṛ. 5-44-14)

(ii) May we achieve our desire for prosperity by moral means. We will seek advice from our conscience with a prayerful heart. (Ṛ. 10-31-2)

(iii) The Heaven and the Earth will endure.
The days will continue to be followed by nights.
The waters in the rivers will keep flowing.
The sun will keep rising.
And yet, every living being will come to rest.
While I live, may words of truth guard me and protect me on all sides. (Ṛ. 10-37-2)

(iv) O kind Lord!
May we earn waelth and glory by right means. May our wealth help others achieve glory. (Ṛ. 2-23-15)

(v) Accept, O Dēvas, our oblations and prayers. Grant us that we may be good in three ways; (1) in thought (2) in speech, and (3) in action. (Ṛ. 5-4-8)

(vi) O God! The lord of the universe! the stimulator of good thoughts. We ask you to steer us away from an evil path. Please put us on a course which has your blessing.
(Ṛ. 5-82-5)

(vii) If because of being dull-witted I have travelled the unrighteous path, please have mercy on me, O Lord. Put me on the right path. (Ṛ. 7-89-3)

(viii) Arduous prayers have given birth to truth and righteousness. It is as if the blistering heat has given birth to the cool night and foaming waters of the sea. (Ṛ. 10-190-1)

(ix) O Lord and master of your will!
Give me the strength of determination,
that I may succeed
in moving away from the darkness of untruth
to the light of truth. (Y. 1-5)

(x) O Lord! Fill in us the desire to offer worship to you.
Make us cherish only those desires which are noble.
Make us utter only those words which are pure, clean, and cordial. (Y. 11-7)

(xi) Bar me O Lord, against evil conduct.
Make me a sharer in good conduct.
I have risen up with good life following the angels. (Y. 4-28)

(xii) Inside every human being is a spirited mind; let my spirited mind propel me to noble resolves. Let my actions be like the actions of those active and wise sages who are worthy of emulation. (Y. 34-2)

(xiii) Good actions are possible with the use of stored wisdom, a firm intellect, and the command that comes from the heart, where our soul, the deathless flame, resides.
Let my mind be drawn to noble actions. (Y. 34-3)

(xiv) A skillful charioteer controls his horses with reins in his hands.
A smart man, likewise, controls himself with the reins of his mind.
Let my swift mind propel me to noble resolves. (Y. 34-6)

(xv) Lord, we shall follow the virtuous path steadfastly like the Sun and the Moon follow their paths. We shall associate with the generous, the kind, and the learned. (Ṛ. 5-51-15)

(xvi) For us, your worshippers who live righteously O Lord, let the breeze be fragrant; let waters in the rivers be sweet; let the herbs be potent; let our days and nights be happy; let the mother earth be sweet as honey, let the father heaven be like nectar; let our cows produce for us milk, sweet like honey; and let the sun be pleasant to us. (Ṛ. 1-90-6,7,&8)

Chapter 37

THE WEDDING CEREMONY

(a) Prayer by the Parents of the Bride

Smooth and troublefree be the paths on which our well-wishers travel to attend the wedding ceremony. May the wedding ceremony be smoothly accomplished. May the Dēvas make this union strong. (Ṛ. 10- 85-23)

(b) Blessings to the Bride

(i) O Bride! In the presence of the sacred fire have you been given to your husband. May you live long and may your life be filled with glory. May your husband see a hundred summers. (Ṛ. 10-85-39)

(ii) O Bride!
May your father-in-law treat you as a queen.
May your mother-in-law treat you as a queen.
May the sisters and brothers of your husband treat you as a queen. (Ṛ. 10-85-46)

(iii) Let this bride be attended with good fortune. Before you (the guests) depart for your home, come one and all to meet her and wish her happiness. (Ṛ. 10-85-33)

(iv) O Bride! May your wish for happiness, for children, for financial well-being, and for being blessed, be fulfilled.
Go. Get busy merging your mind with that of your husband and may both of you live long. (A. 14-1-42)

(v) May Dēva Pūṣan himself lead you by hand from here. May the Aśvins carry you in their own chariot. O Bride! Go to your new home to become the ruler of the house, with authority in your voice. (Ṛ. 10-85-26)

(vi) O Bride! May happiness attend you in your new home. May love increase as you bear children. Unite your person with that of your husband and continue to rule over the household all your life. (Ṛ. 10- 85-27)

(b) Blessings to the Bride and Bridegroom

(i) O Bride and Bridegroom!
The angels have united the two of you to make a loving pair.
May you be united in your thoughts and desires;
May you be united in your actions; and
May you together achieve glory. (A. 2-30-2)

(ii) The Lord has made her for you and the Lord has created you for her.
May He grant long life to both of you. (A. 6-78-3)

(iii) O Lord!
Unite this man and this woman in love like a pair of cakravāka love-birds.
May this couple be blessed with children; and
May both be blessed to enjoy the full span of life.(A. 14-2-64)

(iv) O newly married couple!
May you make a stable family, never to separate.
Enjoy the full span of life, happy, sporting with children and grandchildren. (Ṛ. 10-85-42)

(c) Statements by the Bride and Groom

(i) I take thy hand in mine for good fortune, that thou mayest live to old age with me, thy husband. Dēvas Bhaga, Aryamā, and the bounteous Savitā have given thee to me, for you to become the ruler of my house. (Ṛ. 10-85-36)

(ii) May all the angels unite our hearts. May the flowing waters unite our hearts. May Mātariśvan and Sarasvatī unite our hearts. (Ṛ. 10-85-47)

I am the man; you are the woman;
I am the song; you are the lyric;
I am the sky; you are the earth;
We two shall make a home;
And, we will bring forth children. (A. 14-2-71)

(iii) May I be sweeter than honey; sweeter than liquorice.
May you long for me – as a honeybee longs for a flower full of honey. (A. 1-34-4)

(iv) May the wind bring to us joy;
May the sunshine fill joy in us;
May our days be filled with joy;
May the nights be gifts of peace;
May the sunrise bring us joy. (A. 7-69-1)

(v) The Almighty Lord has yoked us together in a strong bond. He is the one whose will prevails. May He keep us free (from troubles) through the end of our days. (A. 6-133-1)

(vi) Sweet like honey be the messages we convey to each other with our glances.
May we place each other in our hearts; and
May our minds become one. (A. 7-36-1)

(vii) I am accepting the hand of my life-partner today.
Lord, lead us to the world of supreme bliss and joy,
where I could live with my family;
where adversity and destruction may not follow us.
(A. 12-3-17)

(d) Statement by the Bride to the Groom

I envelope thee in my garment, and declare that thou shalt be mine and mine alone.
Even the thought of other women should not enter your mind.
(A. 7-37-1)

(e) Blessings by Well-wishers

May the Earth and the Heaven be auspicious and troublefree for you;
May the sunshine bring you blessings;
May the wind bring you good luck;
May the rivers bring you plenty of clear water for your good.
(A. 8- 2-14)

May the wind purify you;
May the waters bring you immortality;
May the warmth of the sun bless your bodies;
May death spare you so that you may live long. (A. 8-1-5)

Chapter 38

WELFARE AND PROSPERITY

(i) May the glorious Indra augment our welfare;
May the all-knowing Pūśan augment our welfare;
May Sūrya, the protector from misfortunes, augment our welfare;
May Bṛhaspati, the granter of wisdom, augment our welfare. (Ṛ. 1-89-6)

(ii) The Lord is the savior, the protector, and the almighty whom we joyfully invoke. May He, the magnanimous, confer His blessing on us. (Ṛ. 6-47-11)

(iii) O Generous Lord Indra! You are the father; and you are the mother. We pray for your blessing. (Ṛ. 8-98-11)

(iv) O Lord! Our Friend!
May we, always happy, sound of sight, blessed with family, free of sickness, devoid of sin, worship Thee everyday.
May we continue to witness the rising sun by being granted long life. (Ṛ. 10-37-7)

(v) O lord of all! None except you pervades everything and every being. May our wishes, for which we have come to pray you, be granted. May we become happy and prosperous.
(Ṛ. 10-121-10)

(vi) With the worship of fire, we ask all the Dēvas to come to our home today. We welcome you to our home so that you may help us get rid of all our troubles and evil ways.

(Ṛ. 5-51-13)

(vii) Lord!
You are the protector; protect me.
You are the giver of life; give me long life.
You provide the intelligence; provide me with a sharp mind.
You know what I lack; grant that to me. (Y. 3-17)

(viii) Lord! Let the breeze be propitious to us;
Let the sun shine for our well-being;
Let the thunder bring us the much needed rain. (Y. 36-10)

(ix) God! You are our father. Salutations to you.
May my family win your favor.
Grant us children and animals.
Protect my children, my spouse, and me from all harm.
(Y. 37-20)

(x) To you O Glorious One, we come to pray for the welfare of our friends. Listen to our prayers and keep them away from evil men. (Ṛ. 5-24-4&3)

(xi) May Dēva Mitra, our friend and protector, be propitious to us;
May Dēva Varuṇa, the inspirer of righteousness, be propitious to us;
May Dēva Aryaman, calling for activity, be propitious to us;
May Dēva Indra, calling for valor, be propitious to us;

May Dēva Bṛhaspati, the granter of wisdom, be propitious to us;
May Dēva Viṣṇu, of long strides, who is our preserver, be propitious to us. (Ṛ. 1-90-9)

(xii) Lord, we seek your blessings.
May you as Aśvins bless us;
May you as Bhaga bless us;
May you as Aditi bless us;
May you as Pūṣan bless us;
May you as Heaven and Earth bless us;
May you as Vāyu bless us;
May you as Sōma bless us;
May you as Bṛhaspati bless us;
May you as Ādityas bless us;
May you as Mitra bless us;
May you as Varuṇa bless us;
May you as Indra bless us;
May you as Agni bless us. (Ṛ. 5-51-11,12 & 14)

Chapter 39

WIDOW

Rise up O woman, to the world of the living. Your husband is dead. Take the hand of a new man and start your life again.

(Ṛ. 10-18-8)

A woman may lose her husband to death.
Such a woman may find a new husband and dedicate her love to the newly-found mate. (A. 9-5-27)

Chapter 40

WISDOM

Prayers Seeking Wisdom
(a) Gāyatrī Mantra

(i) (The Earth, the Sky, and the Heaven praise Him.) Let us meditate on the glory of the divine Lord. He is the One who sustains us. We pray to Him that He may direct our understanding by instilling wisdom in us. (Ṛ. 3-62-10)

Commentary

This is the most famous of all Vedic mantras, and is called Gāyatrī mantra after the meter in which it is composed.

(b) Other Mantras

(i) O Dēvas, the rulers of minds!
I do not want a limited growth of my mental powers;
I seek your blessings in my wish for an unimpeded growth of my mental faculties. (Y. 8-21)

(ii) He is the lord of what moves and what does not move. We invoke Him to protect us from what is evil (asat), to save us from decline, and to support us in the growth of our mental abilities. (Ṛ. 1-89-5)

(iii) May the wise Lord keep us all our days on the righteous path and grant us long life. (Ṛ. 1-25-12)

(iv) O God Almighty! I am steeped into the darkness of ignorance. I need to be moved into the light of your wisdom. (Ṛ. 1-50-10)

(v) Lord! We bring to You our adoration!
Lead us through the righteous path to riches.
Lord! You know every sacred duty.
Remove the thoughts from our minds that make us stray and wander. (Ṛ. 1-189-1)

(vi) O Omnipresent Lord! Sharpen my intellect, increase my wisdom, and make me a hard worker so that I may cross over all of life's difficulties. (Ṛ. 8- 42-3)

(vii) O Wise Lord! I ask you to sharpen my mind and grant me wisdom — that kind of wisdom which my ancestors and the angels have sought from you. (Y. 32-14)

(viii) Just as the Lord has firmly established the bright sun in the sky, may He establish the brightness of intellect in me. May I earn glory from good actions. (A. 6-69-3)

(ix) Various pools of water may look alike, but some may be knee deep and others may be much deeper. In the same way most people may appear to be equally endowed with eyes and ears, and yet their natural abilities to absorb wisdom imparted by an instructor may be very different (Ṛ. 10-71-7)

(x) Bring us, O Lord, in touch with a wise person who may rightly direct us; who may say, "This is the way". (Ṛ. 6-54-1)

(xi) One who does not know the way should enquire of one who knows.

Directed by the instructor he achieves his destination. Indeed, the benefit of obtaining instruction is that one may reach there by the straight path. (Ṛ. 10-32-7)

Chapter 41

WORK ETHIC

(i) God! You are disdainful of the lazy.
You are disdainful of the rich person who does not help the poor and the needy.
They both quickly perish. (Ṛ. 1-120-12)

(ii) Men! God has given you the elixir of life. Yet, He is a friend of only those who work hard. (Ṛ. 4-33-11)

(iii) Those who are kilned in the fire of hard work, gain maturity and receive your blessings, O omniscient and omnipresent Lord. Those immature people who live in sloth do not receive your blessing. (Ṛ. 9-83-1)

(iv) Listen young person!
You have the dynamism needed for personal growth.
You have the ability to fight with injustice.
Go. Get ahead of your compeers.
God bless. (A. 2-11-2)

Appendix 1

The Vēdas - Their Components

There are four sets of Books known as Vēdas. They are Ṛgvēda, Yajurvēda, Sāmavēda, and Atharvavēda. Each of these four consists of several books classified as Saṃhitās, Brāhmaṇas, Āraṇyakas, and Upaniṣads. Except for Yajurvēda, which has two Saṃhitās, the other three Vēdas have only one Saṃhitā each. Each Vēda may have one or more Brāhmaṇas, one or more Āraṇyakas and several Upaniṣads.

Unfortunately the Saṃhitās, Brāhmaṇas, Āraṇyakas, and Upaniṣads are not mutually exclusive books. A Saṃhitā may contain an entire Upaniṣad as part of its text. For example, Īśāvāsya Upaniṣad forms the 40th and last chapter of Yajurvēda (Vājasanēyi) Saṃhitā.

A Brāhmaṇa may include the complete text of the Āraṇyaka of the same name as Aitarēya Āraṇyaka, Taittirīya Āraṇyaka, Śatapatha Āraṇyaka, Chāndōgya Āraṇyaka, Jaiminīya Āraṇyaka, are. Most, but not all, Āraṇyakas are part of Brāhmaṇas. One well-known exception is Kauśītaki Āraṇyaka which is not part of Kauśītaki Brāhmaṇa.

A Brāhmaṇa may include an Upaniṣad. Examples are Taittirīya Upaniṣad (part of Taittirīya Brāhmaṇa?), Bṛhadāraṇyaka Upaniṣad (part of Śatapatha Brāhmaṇa), Chāndōgya Upaniṣad (part of Chāndōgya Brāhmaṇa) and Kēna Upaniṣad (part of Talvakāra Brāhmaṇa).

An Āraṇyaka may contain one or more Upaniṣad. Aitarēya Upaniṣad is part of Aitarēya Āraṇyaka and Kauśītaki Upaniṣad is part of Kauśītaki Āraṇyaka. The following table is a summary of the connections.

The Four Vēdas

Ṛgvēda

Saṃhitā :	Ṛgvēda Saṃhitā
Brāhmaṇas:	Aitarēya Brāhmaṇa
	Kauśītaki Brāhmaṇa
Āraṇyakas:	Aitarēya Āraṇyaka
	Kauśītaki Āraṇyaka
	(Not part of Kauśītaki Brāhmaṇa)
Upaniṣads:	Aitarēya Upaniṣad (part of Aitarēya Āraṇyaka)
	Kauśītaki Upaniṣad (part of Kauśītaki Āraṇyaka)

Kṛṣṇa Yajurvēda

Saṃhitā:	Taittirīya Saṃhitā
Brāhmaṇas:	Taittirīya Brāhmaṇa
Āraṇyakas:	Taittirīya Āraṇyaka
Upaniṣads:	Taittirīya Upaniṣad
	Kaṭha Upaniṣad
	Maitrī Upaniṣad
	Śvētāśvatara Upaniṣad

Śukla Yajurvēda

Saṃhitā:	Vājasanēyī Saṃhitā
Brāhmaṇas:	Śatapatha Brāhmaṇa
Araṇyakas:	Śatapatha Āraṇyaka
	(Part of Śatapatha Brāhmaṇa)

Upaniṣads: Bṛhadāraṇyaka Upaniṣad
(Part of Śatapatha Brāhmaṇa)
Īśāvāsya (The 40th and last chapter of Vājasaneyī Saṃhitā).

Sāmavēda

Saṃhitā: Sāmavēda Saṃhitā
Brāhmaṇas: Chāndōgya, Jaiminīya (Talvakāra) Pañcaviṃśa, Ṣaḍviṃśa
Āraṇyakas: Chāndōgya, Jaiminīya (Talvakāra)
(all parts of respective Brāhmaṇas
Upaniṣads: Chāndōgya Upaniṣad (part of Chāndōgya Brāhmaṇa), Kēna Upaniṣad (part of Talvakāra Brāhmaṇa)

Atharvavēda

Saṃhitā: Atharvavēda Saṃhitā
Brāhmaṇas: Gōpatha Brāhmaṇa
Upaniṣads: Kaivalya Upaniṣad
Māṇḍūkya Upaniṣad
Muṇḍaka Upaniṣad
Praśna Upaniṣad

Appendix 2

The 33 Vedic Deities (Dēvas)

1. **Aditi** - infinity; an atmospheric deity; mother of Ādityas.
   Ādityas - collective name for the six sons of Aditi, who are deities of the heavenly sphere. They are Aṃśa, Aryaman, Dakṣa, Mitra, Savitṛ, and Sūrya. Their function is to punish sin.

2. **Agni** - The priest, the messenger, the angel; also called Vaiśvanara meaning common to all men, and Jātavēdas meaning, "he who knows all created beings".

3. **Aṃśa** - One of the six Ādityas.

4. **Apāṃ napāt** - a terrestrial deity.

5. **Aryaman** - One of the six Ādityas commonly invoked with Indra and Varuṇa.
   Asura - an epithet used for God, meaning mighty or possessor of wonderful powers. The term later began to mean a demon.

6,7. **Aśvins** - Two divinities who appear in the sky before dawn, in a golden carriage drawn by horses. They represent the morning twilight and are the dispellers of darkness. They are also regarded as divine physicians.
   Bhaga - see Savitṛ.

8. **Bhāratī** - the prototype of Lakṣmī, the consort of Viṣṇu.
   Brahmaṇaspati - same as Bṛhaspati

9. **Bṛhaspati** - God of wisdom and eloquence known as Bṛhaspati Gaṇapati. Later the real name was dropped and the epithet Gaṇapati became popular.

10. **Dakṣa** - Dexterous deity; one of the six Ādityas.

11. **Dyaus** - The shining one; the personification of heaven; Dyaus is addressed as Dyaus the father, or Dyaus Pitar, which is the same as Zeus Pater in Greek and Jupiter in Latin.
    Gaṇapati - see Bṛhaspati.

12. **Garutmat or Garuḍa** - e. of Sun in Ṛgvēda, sometimes depicted in the from of an eagle; see also Viṣṇu.

13. **Iḷā** - Goddess of plenty in the Ṛgvēda. In later Saṃskṛta literature Iḷā is the name of Durgā, the goddess of plenty, who is also called Annapūrṇā for that reason.

14. **Indra** - Deity of the middle region; the greatest Vedic deity; killer of Vṛtra — the demon of draught. Also called by various names including Maghavan.
    Maghavan - see Indra.

15. **Maruts** - The storm deity; the deity who sheds rain.

16. **Mātariśvan** - The deity who brings fire to the earth from heaven.

17. **Mitra** - N. of an Āditya generally invoked with Varuṇa; a friend of human beings.

18. **Parjanya** - the rain god; One who strikes evil doers.

19. **Prajāpati** - creator of heaven and earth; the prototype of Brahmā; the father of both dēvas and asuras.

20. **Pṛthivī** - the earth.

21. **Pūṣan** - the lord of all things moving and stationary; guardian of roads; conferer of prosperity.
Ṛbhus - three deified persons.

22. **Rudra** - The strongest and the mightiest deity who is auspicious (Śiva). Rudra bestows blessings and welfare (Śaṃkara).

23. **Sarasvatī** - Deified river; Goddess of wisdom; Sarasvatī is part of the Vedic triad of Sarasvatī, Iḷā, and Bhāratī, who are the prototypes of later Hindu triad of Sarasvatī, Durgā, and Lakṣmī. In later literature Sarasvatī became the goddess of eloquence and learning.

24. **Savitṛ** - One of the six Ādityas; a golden deity sometimes identified with Sun. The famous Gāyatrī Mantra (also called Sāvitrī mantra) praises God as Savitṛ.

25. **Soma** - king of plants; slayer of the wicked; lord of heaven; moon; a beverage.

26. **Sūrya** - the Sun; one of the six Ādityas.

27. **Tvaṣṭṛ** - a terrestrial deity; omniform deity.

28. **Uṣas** - The goddess of dawn.

29. **Varuṇa** - One of the most important Vedic deities; the upholder of physical and moral order; presiding over the night; bestower of rain.
Vāstoṣpati - the lord of our dwelling.

30. **Vāyu** - The God of wind.

31. **Viṣṇu** - In Vēda-Saṃhitās he is identified with the activity of the sun; he strides over the heaven in three paces (rising, culminating, and setting); Viṣṇu does good to mankind; His vehicle is garuḍa or garutmat which originally meant sun, but was later identified as the eagle bird. The Purāṇic idea of Viṣṇu lying on the serpent is a development of the Vedic description of Viṣṇu crushing the serpent Vṛtra in the company of Indra. Viṣṇu later became the most important deity of the new Hindū triad, of Viṣṇu, Śiva, and Brahmā. His function of doing good to mankind became expressed as the preserver and protector of mankind.

32. **Vivasvat** - A deity of aerial sphere.

33. **Yama** - The ruler of the blessed dead in the highest heaven.

Appendix 3

List of Mantras Included & Their Authors

अक्षण्वन्तः कर्णवन्तः	ऋ.	10-71-7	बृहस्पति आङ्गिरस
अक्षेत्रवित् क्षेत्रविदं	ऋ.	10-32-7	कवष
अक्षैर् मा दीव्यः	ऋ.	10-34-13	कवष
अक्ष्यौ नौ मधुसङ्काशे	अ.	7-36-1	अथर्वा
अग्न आ याहि वीतये	ऋ.	6-16-10	भरद्वाज
अग्निः पूर्वेभिर्	ऋ.	1-1-2	मधुच्छन्दस्
अग्निना रयिम्	ऋ.	1-1-3	मधुच्छन्दस्
अग्निम् ईळे पुरोहितं	ऋ.	1-1-1	मधुच्छन्दस्
अग्ने नय सुपथा	ऋ.	1-189-1	लोपामुद्रा + अगस्त्य
अग्ने व्रतपते	य.	1-5	प्रजापति
अचिकित्वाञ्चिकितुषश्	ऋ.	1-164-6	दीर्घतमस्
अचित्ती यच्चकृमा	ऋ.	4-54-3	वामदेव
अथा ते अन्तमानां	ऋ.	1-4-3	मधुच्छन्दस्
अदित् सन्तं	ऋ.	6-53-3	भरद्वाज
अध स्वप्नस्य	ऋ.	1-120-12	कक्षीवन्त्
अनुव्रतः पितुः पुत्रो	अ.	3-30-2	अथर्वा
अनृक्षरा ऋजवः सन्तु	ऋ.	10-85-23	सूर्या ऋषिका
अनेहो दात्रम्	ऋ.	1-185-3	लोपामुद्रा + अगस्त्य
अन्ति सन्तं न	अ.	10-8-32	कुत्स
अन्या वो अन्याम्	ऋ.	10-97-14	भिषक्
अभयं द्यावापृथिवी	अ.	6-40-1	अथर्वा
अभयं नः करत्यन्तरिक्षम्	अ.	19-15-5	अथर्वा
अभयं मित्राद् अभयम्	अ.	19-15-6	अथर्वा
अभित्वा मनुजातेन	अ.	7-37-1	अथर्वा
अभ्यूर्णोति यन्	ऋ.	8-79-2	कृत्नु
अमोऽहम् अस्मि	अ.	14-2-71	सूर्या सावित्री
अर्यम्यं वरुण	ऋ.	5-85-7	अत्रि भौम

अश्विना सारघेण मा	अ.	6-69-2	अथर्वा
अस्माकम् अग्ने अध्वरं	ऋ.	5-4-8	वसुश्रुत
अस्य देवस्य मीलहुषो	ऋ.	7-40-5	वसिष्ठ
आ नो भद्राः क्रतवोयन्तु	ऋ.	1-89-1	गोतम राहूगण
आपो हि ष्ठा मयो भुवस्	ऋ.	10-9-1	त्रिशिरस्
आपः पृणीत भेषजं	ऋ.	10-9-7	त्रिशिरस्
आ भारती भारतीभिः	ऋ.	3-4-8	विश्वामित्र
आशासाना सौमनसं	अ.	14-1-42	सूर्या सावित्री
आ हि ष्मा सूनवे	ऋ.	1-26-3	शुनःशेप
इदम् आपः प्र वहत	ऋ.	1-23-22	मेधातिथि
इदं विष्णुर् वि चक्रमे	ऋ.	1-22-17	मेधातिथि
इदाह्नः पीतिमुत	ऋ.	4-33-11	वामदेव
इन्द्रो दीर्घाय चक्षस	ऋ.	1-7-3	मधुच्छन्दस्
इन्द्रं मित्रं वरुणम्	ऋ.	1-164-46	दीर्घतमस्
इन्द्र श्रेष्ठानि द्रविणानि	ऋ.	2-21-6	गृत्समद
इमं मे वरुण	ऋ.	1-25-19	शुनःशेप
इमा आपः प्र	अ.	3-12-9	ब्रह्मा
इमामग्ने शरणिं	अ.	3-15-4	अथर्वा
इमां धियं शिक्षमाणस्य	ऋ.	8-42-3	अर्चनानस आत्रेय
इयं विसृष्टिर् यत आ बभूव	ऋ.	10-129-7	प्रजापति परमेष्ठी
इह प्रियं प्रजया	ऋ.	10-85-27	सूर्या ऋषिका
इहेमाव् इन्द्र सं	अ.	14-2-64	सूर्या सावित्री
इहैव ध्रुवां नि	अ.	3-12-1	ब्रह्मा
इहैव स्तं मा	ऋ.	10-85-42	सूर्या ऋषिका
उत त्वं सख्ये स्थिरपीतम्	ऋ.	10-71-5	बृहस्पति आङ्गिरस
उत स्वया तन्वा	ऋ.	7-86-2	वसिष्ठ
उतेयं भूमिर् वरुणस्य	अ.	4-16-3	ब्रह्मा
उदीरतां सूनृता	ऋ.	1-123-6	कक्षीवन्त्
उदीर्ष्व नारयभि	ऋ.	10-18-8	सङ्कुसुक
उद्बुध्यस्वाग्ने प्रति	य.	15-54	अग्नि
उद्यानं ते पुरुष	अ.	8-1-6	ब्रह्मा

उद्वयं तमसस्	ऋ.	1-50-10	प्रस्कन्व
उपत्वाग्ने दिवे दिवे	ऋ.	1-1-7	मधुच्छन्दस्
उप त्वा नमसा	अ.	3-15-7	अथर्वा
उभा शं सा	ऋ.	1-185-9	लोपामुद्रा + अगस्त्य
उरुं नो लोकम्	ऋ.	6-47-8	गर्ग
उरुष्या णो अभिशस्तेः	ऋ.	1-91-15	गोतम राहूगण
ऊर्ध्वो नः पाह्यंहसो	ऋ.	1-36-14	कण्व
ऊरवोर् ओजो जङ्घयोर्	अ.	19-60-2	ब्रह्मा
ऋजुनीती नो वरुणो	ऋ.	1-90-1	गोतम राहूगण
ऋतं च सत्यं	ऋ.	10-190-1	अघमर्षण
एक एवाग्निर्	ऋ.	8-58-2	मेध्यः काण्व
एन्द्र पृक्षु कासु	सा.	231	विश्वामित्र
कतरा पूर्वा	ऋ.	1-185-1	लोपामुद्रा + अगस्त्य
किं स्विदासीद् अधिष्ठानम्	ऋ.	10-81-2	विश्वकर्भा
कितवासो यद् रिरिपुर्	ऋ.	10-85-8	अत्रि भौम
कियती योषा मर्यतो	ऋ.	10-27-12	वसुक
केतुं कृण्वन्न्	ऋ.	1-6-3	मधुच्छन्दस्
को अद्धा वेद	ऋ.	10-129-6	प्रजापति परमेष्ठी
क्रत्वः समह दीनता	ऋ.	7-89-3	वसिष्ठ
क्रत्वा दा अस्तु	ऋ.	6-16-26	भरद्वाज
गणानां त्वा... प्रियाणां...	य.	23-19	प्रजापति
गणानां त्वा... कविं कवीनाम्...	ऋ.	2-23-1	गृत्समद्
गिरयस् ते पर्वता	अ.	12-1-11	अथर्वा
गृभ्णामि ते सौभगत्वाय	ऋ.	10-85-36	सूर्या ऋषिका
गोभिष्टरेममतिं	ऋ.	10-43-10	कृष्ण आङ्गिरस
चक्षुस् त आ प्यायतां	य.	6-15	मेधातिथि
चत्वारि वाक् परिमिता	ऋ.	1-164-45	दीर्घतमस्
जीवेम शरदः शतं	अ.	19-67-1/8	ब्रह्मा
ज्यायस् वन्तश् चित्तिनो	अ.	3-30-5	अथर्वा
तच् चक्षुर् देवहितं	य.	36-24	अथर्वण
तत् सवितुर् वरेण्यम्	ऋ.	3-62-10	विश्वामित्र

तदस्य प्रियमभि	ऋ.	1-154-5	दीर्घतमस्
तदेवाग्निस् तदादित्यस्	य.	32-1	स्वयम्भू ब्रह्म
तद् विष्णोः परमं	ऋ.	1-22-20	मेधातिथि
तनूपा अग्नेसि	य.	3-17	अवत्सार
तम् आसीत् तमसा	ऋ.	10-129-3	प्रजापति परमेष्ठी
तम् इदं निगतं	अ.	13-14-12 & 13	ब्रह्मा
तम् ईशानं जगतस्	ऋ.	1-89-5	गोतम राहूगण
तं त्वा शोचिष्ठ	ऋ.	5-24-4 & 3	गौपायना गौपायन
तवोतिभिः सचमाना	ऋ.	5-42-8	अत्रि भौम
तस्मा अरं गमाम वो	ऋ.	10-9-3	त्रिशिरस्
तस्माद् वै विद्वान्	अ.	11-8-32	कौरुपथि
तुभ्यं वातः पवतां	अ.	8-1-5	ब्रह्मा
तेजोऽसि तेजोमयि	य.	19-9	आभूति
त्राता नो बोधि	ऋ.	4-17-17	वामदेव
त्रातारम् इन्द्रम् अवितारम्	ऋ.	6-47-11	गर्ग
त्रातारो देवा अधि	ऋ.	8-48-14	प्रगाथ
त्र्यम्बकं यजामहे	ऋ.	7-59-12	वसिष्ठ
त्वमग्ने प्रमतिस् त्वं	ऋ.	1-31-10	हिरण्यस्तूप
त्वमङ्ग प्रशंसिषो	ऋ.	1-84-19	गोतम राहूगण
त्वादत्तेभी रुद्र शं	ऋ.	2-33-2	गृत्समद
त्वं स्त्री त्वं पुमान्	अ.	10-8-27	कुत्स
त्वं हि नः पिता	ऋ.	8-98-11	नृमेध
त्वं हि विश्वतोमुख	ऋ.	1-97-6	कुत्स
त्वष्टा जायाम	अ.	6-78-3	अथर्वा
दक्षिणावताम् इद् इमानि	ऋ.	1-125-6	कक्षीवन्त्
दृते दृ ह मा	य.	36-18	अथर्वण
दृष्ट्वा रुपे व्याकरोत्	य.	19-77	प्रजापति
देव सवितः प्र	य.	11-7	प्रजापति
देवा गातु विदो	य.	8-21	अत्रि भौम
देवानां भद्रा सुमतिर्	ऋ.	1-89-2	गोतम राहूगण
देवान्वा यच् चकृमा	ऋ.	1-185-8	लोपामुद्रा + अगसत्य

दैवी पूर्तिर् दक्षिणा	ऋ.	10-107-3	दिव्य
द्वेष्टि श्वश्रूरप	ऋ.	10-34-3	कवष
न किरस्य शचीनां	ऋ.	8-32-15	मेधातिथि
न किरस्य सहन्त्य	ऋ.	1-27-8	शुनःशेप
न ता मिनन्ति मायिनो	ऋ.	3-56-1	प्रजापति वैश्वामित्र
न तं विदाथ य इमा	ऋ.	10-82-7	विश्वकर्मा
न मा मिमेथ	ऋ.	10-34-2	कवष
न मृत्युर् आसीद्	ऋ.	10-129-2	प्रजापति परमेष्ठी
न मृषा श्रान्तं	ऋ.	1-179-3	लोपामुद्रा + अगस्त्य
नमः शम्भवाय च	य.	16-41	प्रजापति परमेष्ठी
नमः सायं नमः प्रातर्	अ.	11-2-16	अथर्वा
न वा उ देवाः	ऋ.	10-117-1	भिक्षु
न वै वातश् च	अ.	9-2-24	अथर्वा
न स स्वो दक्षो	ऋ.	7-86-6	वसिष्ठ
नाष्टमो न नवमो	अ.	13-4-15/21	ब्रह्मा
नासद् आसीन्	ऋ.	10-129-1	प्रजापति परमेष्ठी
नि काव्या वेधसः	ऋ.	1-72-1	पराशर
परिचिन् मर्तो द्रविणं	ऋ.	10-31-2	कवष
परि त्वा गिर्वणो	ऋ.	1-10-12	मधुच्छन्दस्
परिमाग्ने दुश्चरिताद्	य.	4-28	वत्स
पवित्रं ते विततं	ऋ.	9-83-1	पवित्र
पितानोऽसि पिता नो	य.	37-20	अथर्वण
पुत्रिणा ता कुमारिणा	ऋ.	8-31-8	मनु वैवस्वत
पुनः पत्नीम्	ऋ.	10-85-39	सूर्या ऋषिका
पुनन्तु मा देवजनाः	य.	19-39	वैखानस
पूषा त्वेतो नयतु	ऋ.	10-85-26	सूर्या ऋषिका
पृथिवी शान्तिर् अन्तरिक्षं	अ.	19-9-14	वसिष्ठ
प्रजापतिर् जनयति	अ.	7-20-1	अथर्वा
प्रजापते न त्वदेतान्यन्यो	ऋ.	10-121-10	हिरण्यगर्भ
प्र तद्दुःशीमे	ऋ.	10-93-14	तन्व
प्राच्या दिशः शालाया	अ.	9-3-25/31	भृगु अङ्गिरस्

बृहत् सुम्नः प्रसवीता	ऋ.	4-53-6	वामदेव
बृहस्पते अतियद्	ऋ.	2-23-15	गृत्समद
बृहस्पते प्रथमं	ऋ.	10-71-1	बृहस्पति आङ्गिरस
बृहस्पते सवितर्	य.	27-8	प्रजापति
भद्रं कर्णेभिः श्रृणुयाम	ऋ.	1-89-8	गोतम राहूगण
(भूर् भुवः स्वः) तत्सवितुर्	ऋ.	3-62-10	विश्वामित्र
भूरसि भूमिरस्य दितिरसि	य.	13-18	त्रिशिरा
मधुनक्तम् उतोषसो	ऋ.	1-90-7	गोतम राहूगण
मधुमन् मे निक्रमणं	अ.	1-34-3	अथर्वा
मधुमान् नो वनस्पतिः	ऋ.	1-90-8	गोतम राहूगण
मधुवाता ऋतायते	ऋ.	1-90-6	गोतम राहूगण
मधोर्अस्मि मधुतरो	अ.	1-34-4	अथर्वा
मनो मे तर्पयत	य.	6-31	मधुच्छन्दस्
मन्ये त्वा यज्ञियं	ऋ.	8-96-4	द्युतानो
मयि वर्चो अथो	अ.	6-69-3	अथर्वा
मह्यं यजन्तु	ऋ.	10-12-4	विहव्य
मा पृणन्तो	ऋ.	1-125-7	कक्षीवन्त्
मा भ्राता भ्रातरं	अ.	3-30-3	अथर्वा
माहं मघोनो वरुण	ऋ.	2-27-17	कूर्म
मूर्धाऽसि राड् ध्रुवाऽसि	य.	14-21	विश्वदेव
मोघम् अन्नं	ऋ.	10-117-6	भिक्षु
य आत्मदा बलदा	ऋ.	10-121-2	हिरण्यगर्भ
यः समाम्यो 3 वरुणो	अ.	4-16-8	ब्रह्मा
य इमा देवो	अ.	6-133-1	अगस्त्य
य ईशिरे भुवनस्य	ऋ.	10-63-8	गय
यः प्राणतो निमिषतो	ऋ.	10-121-3	हिरण्यगर्भ
यतो-यतस् समीहसे	य.	36-22	अथर्वण
यत् प्रज्ञानम् उत	य.	34-3	शिवसङ्कल्प
यत्रा नन्दाश्च	ऋ.	9-113-11	कश्यप
यथा वशन्ति	ऋ.	8-28-4	मनु वैवस्वत
यद् अन्तरिक्षं पृथिवीम्	अ.	6-120-1	कौशिक

यद् आशसा	ऋ.	10-164-3	प्रचेतस्
यद् वदामि मधुमत्	अ.	12-1-58	अथर्वा
यशो मा द्यावा	सा.	611	वामदेव गौतम
यस् तित्याज	ऋ.	10-71-6	बृहस्पति आङ्गिरस
यस् तिष्ठति चरति	अ.	4-16-2	ब्रह्मा
यस्त्वा हृदा कीरिणा	ऋ.	5-4-10	वसुश्रुत
यस्मान्न ऋते	ऋ.	2-12-9	गृत्समद
यस्मिन् भूमिर्	अ.	10-7-12	अथर्वा
यस्य कुर्मो गृहे	य.	17-52	अप्रतिरथ
या ते अग्ने पर्वतस्येव	ऋ.	3-57-6	विश्वामित्र
या पूर्वं पतिं	अ.	9-5-27	भृगु
यां मेधां देवगणाः	य.	32-14	मेधाकाम
यावती द्यावा पृ. व. यावद्	अ.	9-2-20	अथर्वा
ये त्रिषप्ताः परियन्ति	अ.	1-1-1	अथर्वा
ये देवानां यज्ञियानां	ऋ.	7-35-15	वसिष्ठ
येन करमाण्यपसो	य.	34-2	शिवसङ्कल्प
येन देवा न वियन्ति	अ.	3-30-4	अथर्वा
येन द्यौर् उग्रा	ऋ.	10-121-5	हिरण्यगर्भ
ये पुरुषे ब्रह्म	अ.	10-7-17	अथर्वा
येषाम् अध्येति	य.	3-42	शंयु
यो जागार तम् ऋच.	ऋ.	5-44-14	अवत्सार
यो नो अग्ने अररिवान्	ऋ.	1-147-4	दीर्घतमस्
यो नः पिता	ऋ.	10-82-3	विश्वकर्मा
यो भूतं च	अ.	10-8-1	कुत्स
यो मृळयाति चक्रुषे	ऋ.	7-87-7	वसिष्ठ
यो वः शिवतमो	ऋ.	10-9-2	त्रिशिरस्
वाङ् म आसन्	अ.	19-60-1	ब्रह्मा
वाजश्च मे प्रसवश्च मे	य.	18-1	देवा
वास्तोष्पते प्रतरणो	ऋ.	7-54-2	वसिष्ठ
वास्तोष्पते प्रति जानीह्	ऋ.	7-54-1	वसिष्ठ
वास्तोष्पते शग्मया	ऋ.	7-54-3	वसिष्ठ

वि चक्रमे पृथिवीम्	ऋ.	7-100-4	वसिष्ठ
विभक्तारꣳ हवामहे	ऋ.	1-22-7	मेधातिथि
वि मे कर्णा	ऋ.	6-9-6	भरद्वाज
विश्वतश् चक्षुर् उत	ऋ.	10-81-3	विश्वकर्मा
विश्वानि देव सवितर्	ऋ.	5-82-5	श्यावाश्व
विश्वाहा त्वा सुमनसः	ऋ.	10-37-7	अभितपस्
विश्वेदेते जनिमा सं	ऋ.	3-54-8	प्रजापति वाच्य
विश्वेदेवा नो अद्या	ऋ.	5-51-13	श्यावाश्व आत्रेय
विष्णो रराटमसि	य.	5-21	औतथ्यो दीर्घतमस्
वेनस् तत् पश्यन्	य.	32-8	स्वयंभू ब्रह्म
व्यनिनस्य धनिनः	ऋ.	1-150-2	दीर्घतमस्
व्रतेन दीक्षाम् आप्नोति	य.	19-30	हैमवर्चि
शतम् इन्नु	ऋ.	1-89-9	गोतम राहूगण
शं च मे मयश्च	य.	18-8	देवा
शं नो देवीर् अभिष्टय	ऋ.	10-9-4	त्रिशिरस
शं नो धाता शम् उ	ऋ.	7-35-3	वसिष्ठ
शं नो मित्रः	ऋ.	1-90-9	गोतम राहूगण
शं नो वातो वातु	अ.	7-69-1	शन्ताति
शं नो वातः पवता	य.	36-10	अथर्वण
शिवे ते स्तां	अ.	8-2-14	ब्रह्मा
सक्तुम् इव तितउना	ऋ.	10-71-2	बृहस्पति आङ्गिरस
स घा नो योग	ऋ.	1-5-3	मधुच्छन्दस्
सङ् गच्छध्वं सं	ऋ.	10-191-2	संवनन
सङ् गच्छस्व पितृभिः	ऋ.	10-14-8	यम
सञ्चेन् नयाथो	अ.	2-30-2	प्रजापति
सत्यं बृहद् ऋतम्	अ.	12-1-1	अथर्वा
सध्रीचीनान् वः सं	अ.	3-30-7	अथर्वा
स नो बन्धुर्	य.	32-10	स्वयम्भू ब्रह्म
स नो विश्वाहा	ऋ.	1-25-12	शुनःशेप
स नः पितेव	ऋ.	1-1-9	मधुच्छन्दस्
समञ्जन्तु विश्वे देवा	ऋ.	10-85-47	सूर्या ऋषिका

सम् अहम् आयुषा	य.	3-19	अवत्सार
समानी प्रपा सह	अ.	3-30-6	अथर्वा
समानी वा आकूति	ऋ.	10-191-4	संवनन
समानो मन्त्रः	ऋ.	10-191-3	संवनन
समेत विश्वा ओजसा	सा.	372	वामदेव गौतम
सं पूषन्	ऋ.	6-54-1	भरद्वाज
सम्राज्ञी श्वशुरे भव	ऋ.	10-85-46	सूर्या ऋषिका
सं वर्चसा पयसा	य.	2-24	सोम
संसिचो नाम ते	अ.	11-8-13	कौरुपथि
सविता पश्चातात्	ऋ.	10-36-14	लुश
सविता प्रसवानाम्	अ.	5-24-1	अथर्वा
सहृदयं सां मनस्यम्	अ.	3-30-1	अथर्वा
सा मा सत्योक्ति	ऋ.	10-37-2	अभितपस्
सुपर्णं विप्राः कवयो	ऋ.	10-114-5	सध्रि
सुमङ्गलीर् इयं	ऋ.	10-85-33	सूर्या ऋषिका
सुषारथिर् अश्वानिव	य.	34-6	शिवसङ्कल्प
सूर्या चन्द्रमसौ	ऋ.	10-190-3	अघमर्षण
स्योना पृथिवि	य.	35-21	मेधातिथि
स्रक्त्योऽसि प्रति	अ.	2-11-2	शुक्र
स्वर्गं लोकम् अभि	अ.	12-3-17	यम
स्वस्तये वायुम् उप	ऋ.	5-51-12	स्वस्ति
स्वस्ति न इन्द्रो	ऋ.	1-89-6	गोतम राहूगण
स्वस्ति नो मिमीताम	ऋ.	5-51-11	स्वस्ति
स्वस्ति पन्थाम्	ऋ.	5-51-15	स्वस्ति
स्वस्ति मित्रा वरुणा	ऋ.	5-51-14	स्वस्ति
हंसः शुचिषद् वसुर्	ऋ.	4-40-5	वामदेव
हिरण्यगर्भः	ऋ.	10-121-1	हिरण्यगर्भ

Appendix 4

Significant Dates

3000 - 1100 BCE.	-	Ṛgvēda composed
2000 - 1100	-	Sāmavēda, Yajurvēda, Atharvavēda
1750 - 1660	-	Śrī Rāma
1150 - 1064	-	Śrī Kṛṣṇa
1100	-	Bhagavad-Gītā sermon delivered; Jaya and original Purāṇa written
1100 - 700	-	Scriptural Upaniṣads composed
3000 - 1600 BCE.	-	Ṛgvēda
2000 - 1100	-	Sāmavēda, Yajurvēda, Atharvavēda
1750 - 1660	-	Śrī Rāma
1150 - 1064	-	Śrī Kṛṣṇa
1100	-	Bhagavad-Gītā sermon delivered; Jaya and original Purāṇa written
1100 - 700	-	Scriptural Upaniṣads composed
800	-	Kapila — Sāṅkhya system
650	-	Bādarāyaṇa — Vedāntasūtra, Vālmīki — Rāmāyaṇa
624 - 544	-	Gautama Buddha
620 - 580	-	Bhagavad-Gītā in written form
617 - 545	-	Vardhamāna Mahāvīra
550	-	Kaṇāda — Vaiśeṣika
500	-	Gautama — Nyāya, Gautama — Dharmasūtra
400	-	Tripiṭaka, Āpastamaba — Dharmasūtra
350	-	Jaimini — Mimāṃsā, Patañjali — Yogasūtra

300	-	Baudhāyana — Dharmasūtra
200	-	Manusmṛti
100	-	Vasiṣṭha — Dharmasūtra
0 - CE.	-	Jesus Christ
200	-	Yājñavalkyasmṛti,
250	-	Mahābhārata (final form), Brahma-purāṇa
350	-	Bhrahma-purāna
400	-	Harivaṃśa
500	-	Matsya-purāṇa, Vāyu-purāṇa
600	-	Brahmāṇḍa-purāṇa
700	-	Bhartṛhari-Nītiśatakam
750	-	Kūrma-purāṇa, Liṅga-purāṇa
806-838	-	Śaṅkara
850	-	Bhāgavata-purāṇa, Mārkaṇḍēya-purāṇa
900	-	Vāmana-purāṇa, Brahmavaivarta-purāṇa
1000	-	Kampan-Irāmāvatāram, Nārada-purāṇa, Varāha-purāṇa, Skanda-purāṇa
1057-1137	-	Rāmānuja
1100	-	Bhaviṣya-Purāṇa
1236 - 1300	-	Madhva
1469 - 1538	-	Nānaka
1486 - 1533	-	Caitanya
1527 - 1610	-	Tulasīdāsa — Rāmacaritamānasa
1600	-	Śiva Purāṇa
1824 - 1886	-	Dayānanda
1836 - 1886	-	Rāmakṛṣṇa Paramahaṃsa

Appendix 5

The Transliteration of Dēvanāgarī Script to Roman Script and Pronunciation

Vowels	Transliteration	Pronunciation, as in
अ	a	canoe
आ	ā	car
इ	i	citizen
ई	ī	clean, partisan
उ	u	push
ऊ	ū	prudent, prune, cool
ऋ	ṛ	chris, brisk, brittle
ॠ	ṝ	screen
ए	ē	pray, rain, rein
ऐ	ai	binocular, right, night
ओ	ō	over, okra, oval
औ	au	crowd, cow, vow, brown
nasal and visarga		
◌ं	ṃ	natural nasal sound before ya, ra, la, va, śa, ṣa, sa, ha
◌ँ	◌ँ	natural short nasal sound
◌ः	ḥ	aha, aloha
Consonants & Nasals	**Transliteration**	**Pronunciation**
क	ka	meek, skill
ख	kha	mikhail, slackhanger
ग	ga	God

घ	gha	loghut
ङ	ṅa	sing
च	ca	church
छ	cha	churchhill
ज	ja	Jack
झ	jha	hedgehog (hejhog)
ञ	ña	Synch
ट	ṭa	true
ठ	ṭha	anthill
ड	ḍa	dog
ढ	ḍha	redhaired
ण	ṇa	twenty
त	ta	thumb
थ	tha	thrill, thrive
द	da	this
ध	dha	with him
न	na	nut
प	pa	pa
फ	pha	uphill
ब	ba	banner
भ	bha	abhor
म	ma	man
य	ya	yacht
र	ra	red, rose
ल	la	leader
व	va	victor, also as in woman
श	śa	sure

ष	ṣa	push
स	sa	saint
ह	ha	hum
ळ	ḷa	(twenty when pronounced tweny)
ऽ	'	(silent called avagraha)
ꣳ or ꣴ	elongated nasal	gum (pronounce u in gum as in put)

Some compound letter forms

क्	+	ष	→	क्ष
ज्	+	ञ	→	ज्ञ
श्	+	ऋ	→	श्रृ
श्	+	र	→	श्र

Use of a Number after a letter

ओ३म् Here 3 signifies that ओ should be elongated for 3 units of time while pronouncing it.